Life Skills for Girls

Unleash Your Inner Superwoman with Over 100+ Practical Abilities on Everything from Decision-Making and Building Friendships to Meal Preparation and Saving

Table of Contents

Introduction Letter to the Girl

Hey you!

Would you like to be a superwoman? Obviously, no one can have super speed or superhuman strength, but you can learn cool skills and abilities that make you the superheroine of your story. Close your eyes and think of all the qualities you wish to have. Are you done? Believe it or not, you will find everything you want in this book.

Who are you? What do you usually answer when people ask you this question? The answer isn't as simple as saying your name. You first need to discover your identity or who you really are. This book will take you on a journey to explore interesting things about yourself.

Do you wish to make friends easily, learn to read body language, and express your feelings? This can be done by learning interesting communication skills and clever techniques to make you a great friend.

Confidence is one of the best qualities any girl can have. Do you want to know a little secret? No one is born confident. Just like ballet or playing the piano, it's a skill you can learn. You will find here tips and techniques that show you how awesome you really are.

So, is that it? No, there are other great skills you will learn in this book. Start reading to find out everything you are looking for and more.

Introduction Letter to the Parents

Dear parent,

Nowadays, everyone is talking about women's empowerment. Women need to have a voice, learn to stand up for themselves, and have high self-esteem. Girls should be equipped with the skills and abilities to be strong, confident, and independent from a very young age.

The best gift to give your daughter is to teach her essential skills so she can succeed in her life's journey. This book has tips and techniques to empower her and inspire character development and growth.

The book teaches girls to explore their strengths, qualities, interests, and values to discover their true potential and the superwoman within.

Even in this day and age, girls are accused of being ruled by their feelings. This stereotype is prevalent and doesn't seem to be going away. Your girl can beat these stereotypes by learning about emotions and how she can manage them. This book defines emotions, explains how they work, and their significance.

Girls will spend their lives socializing, connecting with others, and making friends. However, approaching people and making conversation isn't easy for everyone. Your daughter will learn essential communication skills to handle various social situations. She will also understand the significance of being empathetic and kind and respecting others. All are necessary qualities for building healthy relationships.

A confident girl can take over the world. Thus, this book focuses on the power of self-confidence and shows your daughter that she doesn't need validation from anyone else. She can find her own strength from within.

The book also covers other significant skills like handling money, setting goals, self-care, and how to take care of household chores.

Trust that your daughter can handle the content of this book on her own. However, don't hesitate to provide guidance if she asks for your help.

Section 1: Discovering Your Inner Superwoman

Have you ever looked at your fingerprints? They're one of a kind, just like you! You see, everyone is like a beautiful, unique puzzle piece in the giant puzzle of life. No one else is exactly like you, and that's what makes you special. As you grow up, you'll notice that you're not the same person you were when you were younger. That's because you're also going through a wonderful transformation – *just like how a caterpillar turns into a butterfly*! These years are the cocoon stage of your life. This stage matters a lot because it shapes the amazing person you will become.

Like how a caterpillar turns into a butterfly, you're also going through a wonderful transformation.
https://unsplash.com/photos/black-and-white-butterfly-on-gray-and-white-stone-IC8zpKz6qF0

Your choices and how you treat others right now will shape your future self. Your choices and actions today will grow into tomorrow's beautiful flowers and fruits. So, how do you discover the fantastic person you're meant to be? Well, that's what this chapter is all about. The first step is to uncover your strengths as a superhero discovers their powers. Next, you'll want to identify your values and beliefs. These will be your compass in life, guiding you in making the right choices. You'll learn to decide what's important to you and how to stick to your principles. Don't forget being a superwoman isn't just about what you can do but also how you treat others. That's where good manners, kindness, and gratitude come in.

Personal Strengths and Talents

Everyone is good at different things. And the things you're really, really good at are your strengths and talents. For instance, maybe your sister is great at solving tricky math questions. Or perhaps your friend is super talented at creating beautiful art that makes your jaw drop. But what about you? You also have your own unique talents and strengths!

Why are these strengths so important? Well, knowing your strengths makes you feel strong and confident. They help you find what you love to do and do it well. Also, life sometimes has problems, right? Your strengths are problem-solving tools. They will help you figure things out. They are part of what makes you a superwoman.

However, these strengths are not always obvious. A superhero's powers aren't revealed automatically, so your talents might not be known to you or the world yet. Therefore, think again if you believe you have no strengths or talents. To find out what your strengths are, try the following exercises and activities:

Strength Bingo

If you can't figure out your good qualities, here's a bingo to remind you! Color in the boxes you think define your strengths.

B I N G O

Kindness	Creativity	Friendship	Imagination	Bravery
Curiosity	Good at Listening	Positive	Teamwork	Determined
Responsible	Adaptable	FREE	Patient	Helpful
Caring	Charismatic	Strong	Organized	Open-Minded
Optimistic	Problem-Solving	Reflective	Funny	Authentic

Talent Show

Ask your family and friends what they think you're really good at. Sometimes, they see things you might not see in yourself. Write them down below:

- _____
- _____
- _____
- _____
- _____
- _____

Talent Detective

Choose one adventure you've had: Drawing, Dancing, Singing, or Sports. Write your adventure choice below:

Adventure Choice: _____

- How did your adventure make you feel:

_____

- What did you do during your adventure:

_____

- What did you enjoy the most? What made you feel awesome?

_____

Draw a big star below and write down one amazing thing you learned about yourself during this talent detective challenge.

Exploring Interests and Passions

You know that feeling when you do something, and it makes your heart dance with joy? Maybe you lose track of time while reading a book or get totally lost in a movie. Guess what? Those things you absolutely love doing are your passions, interests, or hobbies (if you do them a lot).

Passions, interests, and hobbies are your personal adventures and are very special. They're the things that make you feel alive, curious, and excited. It could be drawing, playing a sport, cooking, dancing, or anything that makes you happy.

However, you might not always be doing the things you love, and that's okay, too. Maybe you haven't discovered them yet or aren't sure where to start. Sometimes, life gets busy, and people forget to make time for their passions.

Here's the secret to a happy life: you should never hold back from doing what you love as long as it doesn't hurt anyone. Trying new things and exploring your interests can be an amazing adventure. If you haven't found your passions yet, keep exploring. Your interests are waiting for you to discover them; when you do, they'll bring much joy and excitement to your life. Try these exercises to find your passion:

1. Hobbies Inventory

Think about activities that make you happy or curious. These could be things you already enjoy doing or have always wanted to try. Write or draw them in the first column. For example, you can write "Reading," "Drawing," "Soccer," "Cooking," or anything else that comes to mind. In the second column, describe how each activity makes you feel. Does it make you feel excited, relaxed, or maybe even proud? Use words or draw emojis to express your feelings. In the third column, decide if there are any activities you'd like to try but haven't yet. If you're curious about something, write "Yes" next to it. If not, write "No."

Interest/Hobby	How It Makes Me Feel	Want to Try (Yes/No)

Take a moment to look at your inventory. Are there any surprises? Did you discover something new about yourself? Share your list with a family member or friend and discuss your interests and feelings.

2. Passion Worksheet

In the first column, write down or draw symbols for your hobbies and interests. These interests are the seeds waiting to grow into your passions. In the "My Goal" column, write one goal for each hobby or interest. What would you like to achieve or explore related to this hobby? In the last column, jot down simple steps you can take to work towards your goals.

Hobby/Interest	My Goal	Steps to Take

Choose one goal to start with and take one small step today. Every step brings you closer to nurturing your hobby into a passion.

Sometimes, you might ask yourself, "Is this just a fun hobby, or could it be something more?" Well, your interests are not just for fun. In fact, they can be the seeds of your passions and your life's work! Imagine turning your love for something into a journey that lasts a lifetime. Whether you're into art, science, animals, or anything else, your interests can shape your future in incredible ways. Take the example of these two incredible women:

• J.K. Rowling

J.K. Rowling loved to write stories. She had a big idea about a young wizard named Harry Potter and his magical adventures. Even though she faced many challenges and rejections from publishers, she didn't give up on her passion for writing. Eventually, a kind publisher saw the magic in her writing, and her books about Harry Potter became famous worldwide. J.K. Rowling's passion for writing turned into a successful career, and her stories inspired millions of readers.

• Jane Goodall

Another amazing woman named Jane Goodall had a deep love for animals. She dreamt of going to Africa to study them. She saved money and made her dream come true. In Africa, she lived with chimpanzees in the wild, something no one had done before. Jane learned a lot about these incredible creatures and shared her discoveries with the world through books and documentaries. Her passion for animals became her career as a scientist and conservationist, making a big difference in the world.

Personal Values and Beliefs

Did you know that the things you believe in and the values you hold dear are the compass that guides you through life? These principles shape your behavior, your future, and the path you choose for yourself. Your values influence how you act every day. For example, if you believe in kindness, you'll naturally be kind to others. If you value honesty, you'll tell the truth even when it's tough.

Did you know that the things you believe in and the values you hold dear are the compass that guides you through life?
https://unsplash.com/photos/round-white-compass-iDzKdNI7Qgc

What you believe in today can shape your future. If you believe in working hard and learning, you're more likely to achieve your goals. If you believe in helping others, you might choose a career that positively impacts the world. Your values and beliefs are like the stars in your night sky, helping you navigate life's twists and turns. They can guide you toward friendships that reflect your values and careers that align with your passions. For example, if you believe in protecting the environment, you might choose a job related to conservation. If you value creativity, you might pursue a career in art, music, or writing.

Sometimes, life presents you with tough choices. Your values can be your trusted advisors in these moments. They help you decide what's right for you, even when it isn't easy. So, think about what truly matters to you. Is it kindness, honesty, courage, friendship, or something else?

1. **My Values and Beliefs Reflection**

In the first column, write down five values or beliefs that are important to you. Examples might include kindness, honesty, bravery, family, or friendship. In the next column, write a short definition of what each value means to you personally. Use your own words to explain why each value matters. In the "Real-Life Example" column, write down a real-life example of a time when you acted in accordance with each belief. For instance, if one of your values is kindness, describe a time when you did something kind for someone else.

In the "Challenge" column, think about situations where it might be difficult to uphold these values. Write down a challenge or scenario for each value that could test your commitment. For example, if honesty is a value, the challenge might be, "What if your best friend broke something and asked you not to tell anyone?" In the "Solution" column, brainstorm a solution for each challenge that aligns with your value. How would you handle the situation while staying true to your beliefs? Write down your solutions.

Values	Definition	Real-Life Example	Challenge	Solution

2. Living Your Values

In the first column, write down three values most important to you. In the other column, describe specific actions or behaviors that show how you can live out each belief in your daily life. For example, if one of your values is kindness, you might write, "Help a friend in need" or "Say something nice to someone every day."

Values/ Beliefs	How I Can Live This Value

Take a moment to reflect on how living these values can shape your behavior, decisions, and interactions with others. Think about how these values can guide you on your life's adventures.

Setting Goals and Ambitions

Goals are what you want to accomplish, whether they're big or small. Goals give you a sense of purpose and direction. They are a compass guiding you through uncharted lands. They help you focus your energy and effort on things that matter to you.

Imagine the most exciting things you want to do in the future. It could be becoming a scientist, traveling the world, learning to play an instrument, or making new friends. Big goals can feel overwhelming, so break them into smaller, manageable steps. Create a plan by listing the steps you need to take to reach your goal. Start working on your goals one step at a time. With each step, you get closer to your dreams. Sometimes, the path might be bumpy – but believe in yourself and keep going.

Ambitions are big, exciting things you want to achieve in the long run. Ambitions can be your life's purpose, like becoming a doctor to help others or an artist to inspire the world. Ambitions give your life a grand adventure plot. They shape the kind of person you want to become and the impact you want to make on the world.

1. SMART Goals

SMART is a special tool that helps you create clear, achievable, and exciting goals.

SMART goals are effective when it comes to personal growth.

Dungdm93, CC BY-SA 4.0 <https://creativecommons.org/licenses/by-sa/4.0>, via Wikimedia Commons: https://commons.wikimedia.org/wiki/File:SMART-goals.png

- ### S - Specific

Your goal should be super clear and specific. Imagine telling a friend exactly what you want to achieve, and they totally get it. It's like saying, "I want to read 10 exciting adventure books by the end of the year."

- ### M - Measurable

You need a way to track your progress, just like marking off places on your map. Your goal should be something you can measure, like counting how many adventure books you've read.

- **A - Achievable**

Think about what you can achieve. Your goal should be challenging but doable. If you read one book a month, reading 10 books in a year is achievable.

- **R - Relevant**

Your goal should matter to you and fit into your adventure story.

- **T - Time-Bound**

Set a deadline for your goal, like a quest with a time limit. When do you want to complete it? By the end of the year? By your next birthday? This helps keep you on track.

Your SMART Goal:

Specific: _____

Measurable: _____

Achievable: _____

Relevant: _____

Time-Bound: _____

2. **Time Management**

Time management is about using time wisely to achieve your goals and enjoy your adventures. Plan your time so you can fit in everything you want to do, from studying and playing to exploring new hobbies. Use this table to plan your time well:

Time	Activity

Good Manners

Good manners are about being polite and showing respect to people. It's using nice words, being considerate, and treating others how you want to be treated. They are important because they help you build positive relationships with others. When you're polite and respectful, people enjoy being around you, making your interactions smoother. Good manners include respecting others' feelings and understanding their point of view. It's about being kind and patient.

Remember the Golden Rule – "Treat others as you want to be treated." Good manners involve saying "please" and "thank you," using polite words like "excuse me" and "sorry," and showing gratitude. Good manners also include being a good listener and patient when others talk. Take a look at these scenarios, and practice your manners:

- **Scenario 1 - Saying Thank You:**

Imagine someone has just given you a gift. Write a thank-you note or draw a picture to express your gratitude. Practice saying "thank you" in a thoughtful way.

- **Scenario 2 - Sharing and Politeness:**

Pretend you're having a meal with a friend or family member. Set up a pretend table with play food. Practice using good table manners: using utensils, not talking with your mouth full, and politely asking to pass items.

- **Scenario 3 - Active Listening:**

Talk with a friend, family member, or even a stuffed animal. Practice active listening by paying close attention to what they say and responding thoughtfully.

- **Scenario 4 - Polite Words:**

Create a list of scenarios where polite words are needed, like asking for help, apologizing, or showing appreciation.

- **Scenario 5 - Respectful Behavior:**

Imagine you accidentally bump into someone in a crowded area. Practice saying "Excuse me" and showing understanding. Think about how you would handle the situation politely.

- **Scenario 6 - First Impressions:**

Pretend you're meeting someone new, like a new classmate or neighbor. Practice introducing yourself with a friendly smile and a polite greeting.

- **Scenario 7 - Gratitude Journal:**

Keep a gratitude journal for a week. Each day, write down three things you're thankful for.

Always remember, you're a star in the night sky, shining in your own way. As the wise Dr. Seuss said, "Today you are you, that is truer than true. There is no one alive who is youer than you!" So, as you go on your adventure of becoming the best version of yourself, always remember to be kind, curious, and brave.

Section 2: Managing Big Emotions

You have probably heard your parents and teachers mention the word "emotions" or describe someone as "being emotional." Have you ever asked yourself what emotions are? It is another word for feelings, right? Actually, no.

Emotions are different from feelings. Feelings are simple, while emotions are deep and wide, like the ocean. Before learning to express them, you should explore and understand them.

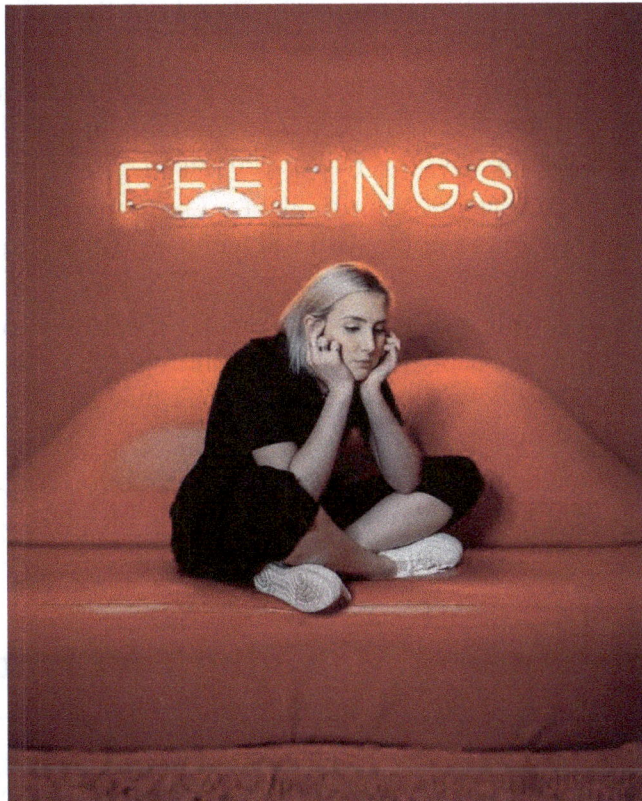

Feelings are simple, while emotions are deep and wide, like the ocean.
https://unsplash.com/photos/woman-in-black-long-sleeve-shirt-and-black-pants-sitting-on-red-couch-h0mKpP_DvWE

When you understand your emotions, you can regulate them. Some emotions can be intense and big, like anger and worry. If you don't know how to manage them, they will control your behavior and make you act unpleasant and unkindly.

This section explains what emotions are, how they work, and what you can do to manage them.

What Are Emotions?

What are you feeling right now? Are you happy, sad, angry, excited, or bored? Whatever you are feeling, these are your emotions. Emotions are your inner feelings, and everything you do is a reaction to them.

Emotions start as a physical sensation or a feeling in your body, and your brain guesses the emotion based on this sensation. Does this sound complicated? Okay, here is an example to simplify it. Suppose your stomach is growling (physical sensation). In that case, your brain interprets this as hunger, and you respond to it by making a sandwich.

Everyone experiences emotions, even babies. Although they can't speak and say how they feel, babies express their emotions by laughing, crying, or hugging.

How Do Emotions Work?

Do you remember the last time you were sad, happy, or scared? What were you thinking when you felt this way? For example, you were going home from school and see the neighbor's dog barking loudly. You think it might bite you, so you feel scared and run.

Or you keep texting your best friend, but she doesn't reply to your messages, so you think she might be mad at you, and you feel sad. Or you haven't seen your grandma in a while, and she hugs you when she sees you. You think she misses you, and this makes you happy.

So, what is the one common thing here? Your thoughts. *Emotions are the results of your thoughts.* If they are positive, like in the grandma example, you will feel happy, but if they are negative, like in the best friend example, you will feel sad.

You create your emotions with your thoughts. If you change them, you can control how you feel. If you believe that your best friend is probably busy and she will reply to your messages soon, you won't be sad. If you think your grandma doesn't love you, it doesn't matter how many hugs she gives you. You will never believe she misses you.

Two people can be in the same situation and have different emotions depending on their thoughts. For example, your mom calls your brother, but he isn't answering his phone. So, she thinks something bad happened to him and feels worried. However, you think he probably put his phone on silent like he always does and will call soon. You feel calmer than your mom.

The Importance of Managing Your Emotions

What happened the last time you were angry? How did you act at this moment? Did you yell or say something hurtful to someone you care about? Sometimes, emotions can be so strong that you can't control your reactions. For example, if your brother breaks your favorite toy, you might cry or yell at him and hurt his feelings. You don't mean anything you say or do, but you can't control your emotions. Later, you find that your brother didn't mean to break your toy, and you feel guilty and say you're sorry. Still, deep down, you wish you had handled the situation better.

Your emotions affect your behavior, mood, and actions. If you are worried or angry, these feelings can affect your schoolwork and your relationship with your family and friends and make you unhappy.

Emotions are manageable. Do all angry or stressed people raise their voices? Of course not. Some can be very angry but remain calm. They don't shout or get mean. They explain their anger and try to find ways to fix the situation.

Remember, you are in control of your emotions, not the other way around. You choose how to react to people and situations that frustrate you. This isn't always easy, but you can learn this skill with the right techniques.

Understand that all emotions are normal. It is OK to feel different types of emotions at once. You can be sad, angry, and frustrated at the same time. Don't ever be ashamed of your emotions; they are part of who you are.

Identifying and Labeling Your Emotions

Sometimes, you can confuse one emotion for another. For instance, one of your classmates invited all your friends to her birthday party except you. When you find out, you start crying and snapping at everyone. Your sister asks you if you are OK, and you tell her you are mad.

Sometimes, you can confuse one emotion for another.
https://www.pexels.com/photo/collage-photo-of-woman-3812743/

17

However, you aren't really angry. You are hurt and sad. Learning to identify and label your emotions can make you feel better. Do you know why? Well, get ready for some cool science facts.

When you feel intense emotions and label them, your brain's thinking part takes over and controls your emotional reactions. In other words, instead of crying or raising your voice, you will react better.

So instead of thinking you are angry and shouting at everyone, you will tell your sister you are hurt and may even cry with her or talk about your feelings.

With the mention of science, you probably think identifying and labeling your emotions is complicated or boring. However, this isn't true. You can learn this skill through some fun and playful techniques.

Emotional Charades

You can play this fun game with your family or friends. Write different emotions on small pieces of paper. Then, put them in a big bowl. Like playing regular charades, you pick a slip of paper, act out the emotion, and let them guess it. Everyone takes turns, and you guess what they are acting.

Read Books

Read picture books that include conflict, emotions, and action. Notice the characters' facial expressions, behavior, and emotional reactions to different situations. Learn vocabulary for the characters' emotions.

You can also watch movies and TV shows and notice the characters' facial expressions when they feel different emotions. You can say it to yourself or out loud whenever you identify an emotion. For instance, if you see a character crying, say, "They must be sad." Ask your parents if there is a facial expression or an emotion you don't understand.

Understand the Emotion Behind Anger

Here is something interesting you may not know about anger. It usually comes as a second emotion. In other words, no one feels angry for no reason. It is usually the result of a negative emotion. For example, you fell while climbing the stairs at school, and other students laughed at you. You feel so embarrassed. Since expressing anger rather than embarrassment is easier, you will hide your true feelings inside and only show signs of anger.

Next time you feel angry, identify and label the main emotions behind your anger. Ask yourself why you feel angry and what triggered this emotion.

Big Emotions Common Triggers

Emotional triggers can be people, situations, or memories that make you feel emotions like sadness, joy, anger, or jealousy. For example, tickling and funny jokes trigger laughter, while sad movies trigger crying.

Identify the common triggers behind big emotions like anger so you can either avoid them or learn to deal with them calmly and healthily.

Check on Yourself

Take a few minutes throughout the day and ask yourself, "How am I feeling now?" If you feel any negative emotion, find out what triggered it. For instance, you checked on yourself and found you were feeling frustrated. Think of everything that happened all day to see what triggered these feelings. When you check up on yourself throughout the day, it will be easier to find the triggers.

Pay Attention to Your Body

There is a physical sensation behind every emotion. When you are angry, you feel hot, your heart rate will increase, and you will breathe faster. When you are afraid, your hands will shake, you will sweat, and you will feel a pain in your chest.

When you feel these physical sensations, you are in a situation triggered by negative emotions. Walk away and find a quiet place to calm yourself down. For example, you are arguing with your best friend, and she says something that hurts your feelings. Suddenly, you feel tense and hot, and it becomes clear you are getting angry. If you continue fighting with her, you might say something hurtful, and things could worsen. You might never speak to each other again.

The best thing to do here is to walk away from your friend. Practice breathing exercises or think of better ways to respond to the situation. Then you can calmly talk to her and explain that she hurt your feelings. You will talk things out and calmly solve your problem.

Pay attention to how your body reacts to different emotions and situations. Teach yourself to take a break from the things that trigger big emotions. This will give you the chance to clear your head and think clearly.

Emotional Regulation Techniques

Breathing Exercise #1

Teach yourself to take a break from the things that trigger big emotions.
https://www.pexels.com/photo/sportive-woman-with-bicycle-resting-on-countryside-road-in-sunlight-3771836/

Instructions:

1. Find a quiet room in your home.
2. Sit down in a comfortable chair.

3. Breathe in and out at a normal pace.

4. When breathing out, make an "aaaaa" sound.

5. Keep doing this exercise until you feel calmer.

Breathing Exercise #2

Instructions:

1. Lie on your back and put one hand on your stomach and the other on your chest.

2. Take a deep breath and feel your stomach expanding with air.

3. Breathe out and feel all the air in your body released and your stomach getting smaller.

4. Notice how the hand on your stomach moves more than the hand on your chest.

5. Repeat until you feel better.

Breathing Exercise #3

Instructions:

1. Take a deep breath through your nose.

2. Breathe out through your lips.

3. Repeat until you feel calm.

You can practice this simple breathing technique when you are in a triggering situation.

Mindful Technique

Instructions:

1. Take a deep breath and look around the room.

2. Name five things you can see in the room.

3. Name four things you can touch or feel.

4. Name three things you can hear.

5. Name two things you can smell.

6. Name one thing you can taste.

Expressing Big Emotions

You can never avoid intense or big emotions. They are a part of life. However, you can learn healthy ways to express and release them.

Art

If you love drawing, this exercise is for you. Whenever you experience intense emotions, draw what you feel. You can draw a young girl who is sad or angry or draw a picture of what you think your emotions look like. Your drawing doesn't have to be perfect. Just focus on the experience and relaxation you feel.

Write a Story

Write a story about a girl going through the same experience or situation as you. Describe her big emotions and what she does to get through them. Give your story a happy ending where the girl conquers negative emotions and becomes happier and more positive. Let your imagination run wild with this story.

Journaling

Sit in a quiet room with your journal and write down all your thoughts and emotions. Write everything you feel, even your embarrassing or most vulnerable moments. Be as honest as you can. This is your journal, and no one will read it but you, so don't hold anything back.

Journaling is a great technique to release intense emotions, and you will feel better and lighter for doing it. You can also wait a couple of days, read what you wrote, and ask yourself questions like the following:

- Do I still feel this way?
- Does this issue still bother me?
- Have the last few days made me calmer?

Keep a journal next to your bed, and make it a habit to write every night about your day and how every situation and person made you feel.

Music

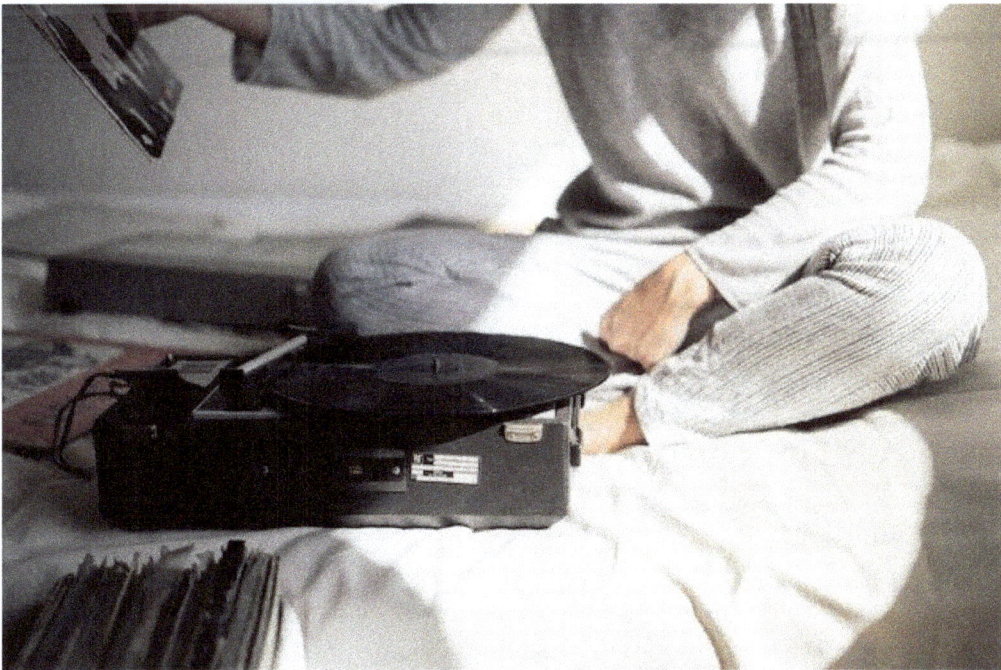

Music can make everything better and heal you from negative emotions.
https://www.pexels.com/photo/person-in-gray-sweater-holding-black-vinyl-record-player-3618362/

Music can make everything better and heal you from negative emotions. Learn to play an instrument like the piano or guitar and use it to express yourself artistically. You can also sing while playing. You don't need to be a pro. Just have fun and release your intense emotions.

Exercise

There are many health benefits of exercising. It is good for your heart, body, and mind. It is a great way to lose weight, protects you from disease, and boosts your energy. Exercising also helps you deal with big emotions like worry and anger. You can exercise any way you want, like swimming, running, rock climbing, punching a bag, etc.

Resilience and Self-Compassion

You know the importance of being kind to everyone you meet, but do you know you should also be kind to yourself? Self-compassion is treating yourself with love, kindness, and understanding. It helps you understand that everyone makes mistakes and faces difficulties, so you should always forgive yourself.

Teach yourself to be resilient so you can recover fast from failures. Life can be hard sometimes, and resilient girls know that better than anyone. They have the right skills and abilities to get back on their feet after every challenge and encourage themselves to keep going until they achieve all their goals.

Repeat Affirmations

Affirmations are powerful, short phrases that can change the way you think. Repeat this every day:

- I forgive myself for my past mistakes.
- I love myself for who I am.
- I am perfect the way I am.
- I treat myself with kindness.
- I celebrate myself every day.
- I deserve respect and love.
- I can pick myself up whenever I fall.
- I am in charge of my emotions.
- I can overcome any setbacks.
- I believe in myself.

Learn Independence

Resilient girls are strong and independent. Learn to stand up for yourself, solve your problems, and try new things within reason. Don't run to your parents whenever you make mistakes. Find ways to fix the situation yourself. Of course, you can always ask for help from your parents or friends, but this should be your plan B.

Treat Yourself with Kindness

Pay attention to your thoughts and how you talk about yourself. For instance, if you get a bad grade, instead of saying, "I am not as smart as the other girls in my class," Forgive yourself and say, "I did my best. I will study harder and get a better grade next time because I am smart and capable."

Don't use harsh or negative words when you talk to or about yourself. Treat yourself the same way you would treat your best friend, brother, or sister. If your best friend comes to you crying and tells you she got a bad grade, will you tell her she isn't smart enough? Of course not. Whatever you tell her, use the same words to encourage yourself whenever you fall.

Friendly Reminder

Managing emotions isn't always easy, so be patient with yourself. However, if you are facing difficulty, talk to your parents and ask them for advice. There is no shame in asking for help. It actually shows courage and maturity.

Remember, your emotions aren't the boss of you. You are the one in control. You have it in you to make the right choices and react kindly.

Your emotions are a part of who you are. Don't ignore the ones you don't like. Just like happiness, anger is an essential emotion you should understand and learn to express healthily.

Love yourself and treat yourself with kindness because you are awesome and deserve to be loved and respected.

Section 3: Communication Skills

"Communication is key." You will hear this sentence throughout your life. You must learn how to communicate with others to have healthy and successful relationships. Imagine life if you could easily talk to people, start a conversation with your classmates, and make new friends. It would be great, right?

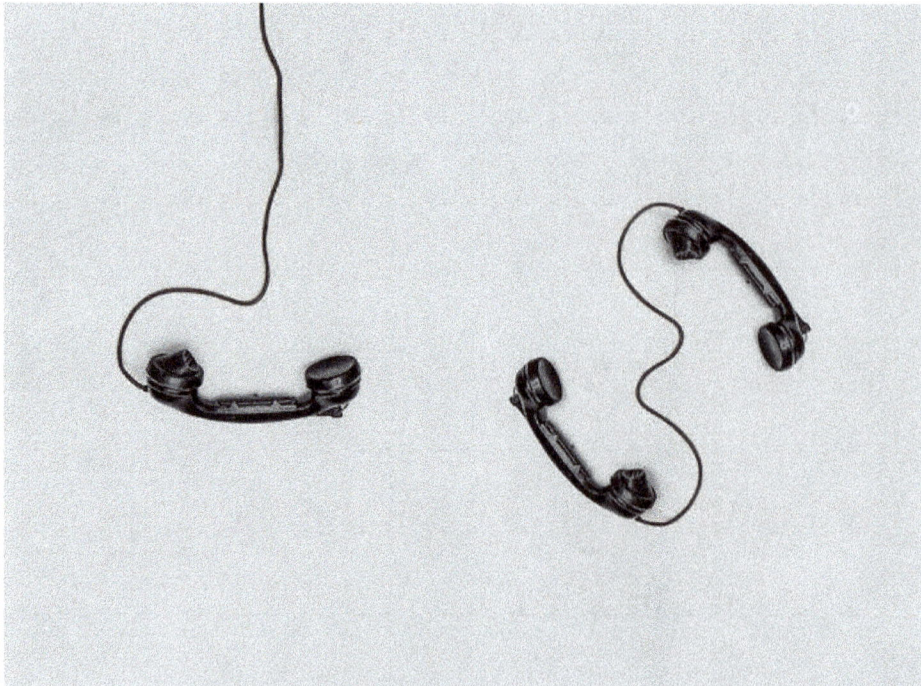

You must learn how to communicate with others to have healthy and successful relationships.
https://www.pexels.com/photo/three-black-handset-toys-821754/

Communication skills will make your life much easier and make you popular. Your friends will love talking to you and spending time with you because you are a good listener and understand them.

Learning communication skills isn't difficult. This section will teach you cool skills like active listening, body language, and conflict resolution.

What Is Communication?

Communication is sharing feelings, thoughts, ideas, and information with others. People usually communicate through talking, listening, and texting. A good communicator should give you all their attention, respect different opinions, speak softly without raising their voice, and ensure that their message is clear and to the point to avoid misunderstandings.

Everything you say and do is a form of communication, even the posts and memes you share online. They reflect who you are and how you want your family and friends to see you. Strong communication skills make texting, using social media, chatting with friends online, and having face-to-face conversations easier.

Different Types of Communication

You usually pay attention to their words when you talk to someone, right? What people say (verbal communication) is important. However, there are many things that people don't say out loud during a conversation but will show in their body language. It is probably the most honest part about them since words can lie, but a person's facial expression will always tell the truth.

Verbal Communication

Verbal communication isn't just what you say during a conversation but how you say it. Your tone, voice pitch, and level of formality (whether you speak respectfully or casually) play a big role in expressing your feelings and thoughts. Be careful with how you speak to others, or people might misunderstand you.

For instance, you are having a conversation with your friend, and suddenly you raise your voice. Your friend gets upset and asks you why you are turning this into a fight. You are confused because you didn't say anything wrong and don't understand why she feels this way. The problem isn't with *what* you said but *how* you said it. When you raised your voice, your friend thought you were angry. Your pitch gave her the wrong idea.

You can have the best intentions and say all the right things, but none of it will matter if you raise your voice or speak sarcastically.

Keep your tone of voice soft and friendly. Pay attention to the volume of your voice. Understandably, you will get angry and upset and might raise your voice. This is normal because sometimes your emotions take over, but you should be polite, especially when speaking to someone older than you. Luckily, in the next section, you will learn to manage your emotions so you can calmly express yourself.

Non-Verbal Communication

Non-verbal communication is your body language, facial expressions, gestures, and posture. People can't always control this part of themselves. If you pay attention and really look at them while they are talking, you will discover interesting things about them.

For example, you are hanging out with your friends and notice one of them is acting differently. Even though she is talking normally, you can see that her facial expressions are off, and she isn't smiling like usual.

You find out later that she is upset because her parents are getting a divorce. She didn't want anyone to find out, so she tried to act normal. However, her facial expressions gave her away.

The Importance of Communication

Communication skills are part of your personal and social development. When you effectively communicate with your friends and family, you can express your needs to them. You will also learn to better understand yourself and others.

For example, you had a bad day at school and don't feel like talking to anyone. People who can't communicate their needs might get angry when their parents ask them about their day and yell, "Leave me alone." However, if you have communication skills, you will calmly tell them, "I had a bad day, and I want to be alone in my room, please."

You need communication skills to bond with the people in your life, learn about them, and build healthy relationships. Talking to your friends and family and seeing how they react to things you do and say will give you a better understanding of yourself. For instance, you will only know you are funny when people laugh at your jokes and stories.

Communication can boost your self-esteem and teach you to be a more compassionate and understanding person. Sharing your ideas and thoughts with others, listening to them when they speak, and giving them your attention will improve your relationships. Your friends and family will love talking to you because you make them feel valued and care about their opinions. You will feel more confident when you see how everyone loves talking to you.

Communication skills will improve every area of your life. So, how can you develop these skills? Well, you are about to find out.

Active Listening

Nowadays, people don't really listen to each other anymore. They are either looking at their phones or waiting for the other person to finish talking so they can speak. When was the last time you actually listened to someone? How do you feel when you are talking to a friend, and they are busy texting or checking their phones?

Active listening isn't just hearing what your friend is saying but trying to find the intention and meaning behind their words.
https://www.pexels.com/photo/two-women-having-conversation-on-stairs-1438084/

If you want to improve your communication skills, practice listening. Active listening isn't just hearing what your friend is saying but trying to find the intention and meaning behind their words. It is about fully focusing on the conversation and not letting anyone or anything distract you.

Active listening is a great skill to develop at a young age using these techniques.

Making Eye Contact

Make eye contact when you are talking to someone. It shows the other person that you aren't distracted and are paying attention to what they say. You are probably thinking, this is easier said than done, right? Eye contact doesn't come easy for everyone. Some people feel awkward or shy when they look someone in the eyes. However, there are a few tips to make things easier.

- Don't make too much eye contact, as it can make people uncomfortable.
- Every five seconds, break eye contact and look at any part of their face or look in one eye at a time.
- Don't look down on your lap or the ground because this shows you are bored and waiting for the conversation to end.
- If eye contact is hard for you, you can look at the person's cheeks, nose, eyebrows, chin, or forehead instead.

This may sound complicated, but in time, you will get used to making eye contact, and soon it will come naturally to you.

Show Them You Are Listening

Since most people are often distracted, your friends and family will appreciate it if they know you are listening to them. There are simple things you can do to show them you are paying attention to what they are saying. Smile, nod, or say things like "uh huh" or "yes" to encourage people to keep talking. Don't play with your fingernails or hair, fidget, or look at your watch, or they will think you are bored and want the conversation to end.

Pay Attention to Social Cues

Social cues are non-verbal communication. When talking to someone, try to notice if they are doing something different with their body and face. For instance, are they crossing their arms, smiling, or looking at their watch?

More than half of people's communication is non-verbal. Interestingly, you can learn more about a person by paying attention to what they aren't saying. For instance, you can tell that a person is anxious if they are talking fast or upset if they are lowering their eyebrows.

It is easier to read the body language of someone you know because you will notice when something is different about them. For instance, your best friend starts to talk fast, or your brother suddenly crosses his arms all the time.

You can read people like a book when you learn about body language and the meaning behind different facial expressions and gestures. You will "listen" to what they aren't saying and respond accordingly.

For example, your best friend's parents are moving her to a new school. She tells you how excited she is and can't wait to meet her new classmates and make friends. However, you can tell from her eyes and the rest of her face that she isn't happy and is trying to hide her sadness. Instead of watching her lie to you and to herself, you hug her and tell her it's OK to be sad and that you are here for her.

How to Express Your Emotions

Imagine you are fighting with your best friend, and you tell her, "What you did was awful. You were unkind and said horrible things to me. You are supposed to be my best friend. How could you talk to me this way?"

Now imagine a different conversation where you say, "I feel really hurt and confused about our friendship."

Can you tell the difference between the two? In the first scenario, you pointed the finger at your friend and accused her of hurting your feelings. Naturally, she will feel attacked and try to defend herself, which can turn into a big fight.

In the second scenario, you used "I" statements that focused on your emotions. Here, you aren't attacking your friend. You are talking about your hurt feelings, not her behavior. Your friend will listen to you and calmly explain herself because she can see that you aren't angry at her but feel sad and hurt.

"I" statements are a healthy communication method where you express your feelings, thoughts, and opinions clearly and respectfully. You don't focus on what the person said or did but on how their actions made you feel. This skill allows you to express yourself without blaming the other person and gives them a chance to explain their side without getting defensive.

Using "I" statements is easy. You start with "I feel" and then discuss how their behavior affects you without blaming them. Make sure to focus only on your feelings and don't use the word "You" in the statement.

- Figure out exactly what you are feeling.
- Explain how their behavior made you feel.
- Don't attack them or judge their character.
- Be assertive and empathetic (you will learn about empathy in the next section).

For instance, instead of telling your big sister, "You don't care about my feelings," you say, "I feel sad when my feelings aren't taken seriously." Or instead of telling your friends, "You always leave me out." say, "I feel hurt when I am not invited to hang out. It makes me feel like I am not welcome."

Assertive Communication Tips and Techniques

Assertive communication is standing up for yourself and expressing your needs and feelings directly and clearly while being polite and respectful. It's about being honest without judging others, belittling their opinions, or hurting their feelings.

Be Straightforward

Be straightforward when talking to others and avoid judgments or negative words. For instance, your sister borrowed your jeans and didn't return them. Instead of telling her, "You always take my stuff and never return it. This is so rude." say, "You were supposed to return my jeans last week, but you didn't, and now you have had them for a month." You expressed your feelings honestly and clearly while asking for an explanation and without hurting your sister's feelings.

Don't accuse your sister of taking your stuff and never returning them. Maybe she has forgotten or thought she already returned them. So, give her the chance to explain herself and hear her reasons.

Rehearse before Talking

Speaking your mind isn't always easy. Practice what you want to say in front of a mirror, or create different scenarios and rehearse them with your brother, sister, or friend. You can also write down what you want to say and read it before you speak to the person.

Body Language

Being assertive is all about confidence.
https://www.pexels.com/photo/smiling-girl-in-trendy-outfit-on-street-7788328/

Being assertive is all about confidence. Even if you don't feel this way, pretend to be confident. Copy the body language of an assertive person by making eye contact, standing up straight, not crossing your arms, and having a positive and friendly facial expression.

Conflict Resolution

No one likes conflicts, but you can't avoid them. They can lead to fights, especially when someone becomes stubborn or doesn't want to compromise. You can't always get your way, but you can learn conflict resolution strategies to find a middle ground.

- When you have an argument or a fight with your friends, walk away from the situation before you say something you don't mean and make things worse. Take a few minutes to calm down and think about what you want to say.

- Make sure you and your friend know the conflict and what caused it to avoid misunderstandings. If you don't, you will find yourself bringing up past fights, making the situation worse.

- Talk about what each of you wants and what you don't want so you can have a healthy and successful conversation.

- Think of the best solutions that benefit both of you. Remember, you are in this together. This isn't about winning or losing but finding a way to end the conflict and protect your friendship.

- Disagreements will happen. Learn to respect your friend's different thoughts and ideas and show them that you value their opinion.

Positive Body Language vs. Negative Body Language

You don't have to be an expert to read body language. Some facial expressions are universal, like crying, frowning, and smiling, while there are things that you can pick up by yourself. For example, you can always tell if your parents, brother, sister, and friends aren't being themselves because you know them and can tell when they aren't okay.

So how can you read people you don't know? You need to recognize the difference between positive and negative body language.

Negative Body Language

Negative body language portrays the person closing themselves off from the world around him.
https://www.pexels.com/photo/lonely-girl-sitting-on-a-doorway-236215/

- **Crossed arms:** Aggression, anger, feeling defensive and closed off, lack of confidence, unwillingness to talk.

- **Frowning:** Anger or feeling upset, lost in their thoughts, or focused on what someone is saying.

- **Avoiding eye contact:** Someone is hiding something, feeling guilty or uncomfortable, or lacking confidence, interest, or respect.
- **Crossed legs:** Insecurity, dishonesty, low self-esteem, or discomfort.
- **Foot or finger tapping:** Anxiety, boredom, impatience, not paying attention, low self-esteem, jumpiness, and feeling nervous.
- **Bad posture:** Anxiety, boredom, feeling threatened, or disinterested.

Positive Body Language

Positive body language conveys that the person is ready to take on the world by storm.
https://pixabay.com/photos/woman-kid-rain-leaf-umbrella-1807533/

- **Firm Handshake:** High self-esteem or respect.
- **Sitting Still:** Relaxation or focus.
- **Leaning in to Listen:** It shows the person is paying attention and interested in what you say.
- **Eye Contact:** The person listens to what you are saying and enjoys the conversation.
- **Good Posture:** Being friendly and paying attention.
- **Smiling:** Shows that the person is friendly, open, likable, approachable, and paying attention to what others say. It also means they like and respect the person they are talking to and hope to strengthen their bond with them.
- **Standing up Straight:** Confidence and knowing what you are doing in life.
- **Open Hands with Palms Facing Up:** This person is approachable, open, and honest.

Communication skills can change your life and improve your relationships. Show people you respect them and value their opinions by listening to them. Notice people's body language and figure out what they aren't telling you. Learn the difference between positive and negative body language and always be open and inviting when interacting with others.

Section 4: Making Friends – Relationships

What is friendship, and what does it mean to you? Back in the '90s, there was a popular TV show called "Friends" about six friends in their twenties living in New York. The theme song's lyrics describe friendship: "I'll be there for you like I've been there before. I'll be there for you 'cause you're there for me too."

Life is about meeting new people and making friends.
https://unsplash.com/photos/women-forming-heart-gestures-during-daytime-tSlvoSZK77c?utm_content=creditShareLink&utm_medium=referral&utm_source=unsplash

Life is about meeting new people and making friends. No one can live alone. You need to be around others to talk to them, share stories, and laugh together. You want people to love and support you.

This section teaches you about the power of friendship and how you can be a good friend.

What Is Friendship?

Friendship is a close bond between people who love and care about each other. It is about being kind, honest, loyal, and generous to them. A friend is someone you love spending time with and always have fun with. You can depend on them because you know they will always be there for you.

You can have many friends, but there will always be one person who means more to you than the rest. This is your best friend. You trust them with all your secrets. They feel like family; you know they will be in your life forever.

Value of Friendship

You love your friends, and they love you, right? If you ask your mom, dad, brother, or sister, they will also tell you their friends mean so much to them. So, what makes friendship so special and valuable?

A friend protects you from loneliness and makes you feel needed. When you share your good news with them, they will be happy and celebrate with you. When you are sad, your friend will give you a shoulder to cry on and will not leave you until you feel better.

You don't hide any part of your personality when you are with your friends. You let your true self shine because you know they love and accept you for who you are. They will never make fun of you or make you feel bad when you make a mistake.

They know what you want to say just by looking at you. Whenever you don't feel good enough, a friend will remind you how awesome you are and make you feel great about yourself.

For instance, you don't like math and got a bad grade on the last exam. You are upset because all your classmates got As and Bs. After class, your best friend tells you she got an A and is so happy. She asks you how you did, but you are too embarrassed to tell her.

However, your best friend knows you better than anyone and can tell by the look on your face that you didn't get a good grade. She might tell you, "I know you got a bad grade; it happens. Don't be sad, it was a hard exam. I know you don't like math, and you did the best you could. You will do better next time."

A good friend will teach you to love yourself and see all your amazing qualities. They want the best for you, will give you good advice, and will prevent you from doing things you might regret later. Simply, friends make your life better.

How to Make Friends

Now for the interesting part, don't you wish you could make friends easily? Sadly, you can't drink a magic potion to make talking to people or making friends easier. However, some tricks will help you when meeting new people.

Don't forget to apply the communication skills you learned in the previous section. These are also useful for making friends and building relationships.

Start a Conversation

- You can learn to make friendly conversation by watching TV shows and movies and seeing how the characters talk to each other.
- Smile when talking to someone, and be nice and friendly.

- If you are talking to someone you don't know, introduce yourself by saying something like, "Hi, I am ... (I am in English class with you" or "I am Jack's Jack's sister." If you are talking to someone you know, start the conversation by saying, "Hi, how are you?"

- Don't frown or fold your arms when talking to others.

- Practice active listening, as you learned in the previous section.

- Saying words like "Wow!" "Really?" "No kidding!" or "That's interesting!" show you pay attention to the conversion.

- Nod to show you are listening and interested in what the other person is saying.

- When someone asks you for your opinion, don't reply with "I don't know" right away. Take a moment to think; maybe you can come up with something to say. You can even wonder out loud and say, "I am not sure, but I think..."

Remember always to be yourself. Don't try to be someone you aren't to impress others. People will love you for being real.

Ask Questions

Try only to ask open-ended questions that aren't answered with "Yes" or "No."
https://www.pexels.com/photo/question-marks-on-paper-crafts-5428836/

Ask questions to get to know the other person better, like, "What TV shows are you watching these days?" "What is the last movie you saw?" "How many pets do you have?" Try only to ask open-ended questions that aren't answered with "Yes" or "No." These questions will keep the conversation going and help you get to know each other better.

For instance, instead of asking, "Have you seen the new Little Mermaid movie?" Ask, "What do you think of the new Little Mermaid movie?"

During conversation, ask follow-up questions to show interest in what they are saying. For instance, if they are talking about their dog, you can ask, "How did you adopt your dog?" Or "How long have you had your dog?"

Role Play

Talking to people you don't know isn't always easy. Practice your conversation starters at home in front of the mirror or role-play with your brother, sister, or parents. You can also practice using your dolls or teddy bears.

For instance, you and your sister can pretend you are meeting for the first time and ask each other fun and interesting questions. This will give you the courage and confidence to start talking to girls and boys at your school and make new friends.

Practice Empathy and Understanding

Do you know the saying "Put yourself in someone else's shoes."? This is empathy. Empathy is understanding how another person feels, even if you haven't had the same experience or been through the same situation. In other words, you can imagine what someone is feeling or thinking so you can give them the support they need.

For instance, your best friend is crying because her dog ran away. You have never had a dog before, so you don't understand the bond a person has with their pet. Empathy helps you understand the pain your friend is going through. You feel sad and hurt – as if you are the one who lost something you love.

As a result, you can help her during this difficult time. You will listen to her talk for hours, hug her to make her feel she isn't alone in this, and help her look for her puppy.

Empathy makes you a better friend. When you understand others, they feel seen and heard, which makes people feel comfortable around you – and your friends feel closer to you.

Although they have a similar spelling, empathy is different from sympathy. Sympathy is feeling sorry for what someone is going through, while empathy is feeling their emotions as if they are your own.

It's OK if you aren't empathetic. You can learn this skill with some simple techniques.

Watch Your Parents

Watch how your parents act when they see someone sad or meet someone less fortunate. Notice how they treat them with kindness and understanding. When you are sad, hurt, or angry and go to your parents, how do they react? Copy their behavior and see how they build lasting bonds.

Talk about Your Emotions

Don't be afraid to talk about your feelings. Be open and honest instead of keeping them inside. Try to understand yourself better and discover the reason behind your emotions. For instance, you are afraid of the dark. Instead of just accepting these feelings, explore them and understand their reason.

Ask yourself why you feel this way, what is so scary about the dark, and what you think will happen if you sleep in a dark room alone. Understanding what someone is thinking and feeling is easy when you know yourself and the reason behind your emotions.

Observe Fictional Characters

Observe fictional characters by watching movies and TV shows or reading stories and discussing the characters, their feelings, and actions with your parents, siblings, or friends.

For instance, you can watch Beauty and the Beast and ask these questions:

1. Why did Belle feel different from everyone else in her town?
2. Why wasn't the Beast nice to Belle when they first met?
3. How did Belle feel knowing she wouldn't go home again?

4. Why did Belle love books so much?

5. What made her fall in love with the Beast?

6. What made the Beast fall in love with her?

7. Have I ever felt like an outsider at home or school?

8. Would I make the same choices as Belle?

This is a great way to understand human emotions and learn to put yourself in someone else's shoes.

Take an Acting Class

If you want to understand how empathy works, take an acting class or participate in a school play. It will show you what it's like to be another person with different feelings and thoughts, and you will discover the world from someone else's eyes.

How to Be a Good Friend

Friendship is about give and take. If you want to have good friends in your life, you should learn to become one yourself. So, what makes a good friend?

Offering Support

Good friends always support each other.
https://www.pexels.com/photo/basketball-team-stacking-hands-together-3755440/

Good friends always support each other in achieving their goals and realizing their dreams. Whenever a friend thinks of giving up, you remind them of all their good qualities and that they have it in them to do the impossible. You always cheer them on and rush to be beside them whenever they need you.

Being Reliable

Be the kind of friend that people can count on and trust. When you promise a friend you will help with her homework, you keep your word. If you make plans with her, you follow through even if something better comes along. You never disappoint your friends, and they know that no matter what, you will never fail to be there for them.

Honesty

No one wants a friend they can't trust and who doesn't tell the truth. When your friend asks you a question, they expect you to be honest with them even if the truth is hard. An honest person won't lie to make their friend happy. They will stick to the truth because it's for their own good.

For instance, your best friend shows you the dress she plans to wear for her cousin's wedding. She asks you for your honest opinion. You can see that the dress doesn't look nice, and you know she has prettier dresses.

So, you tell her the truth without hurting her feelings. You say, "I don't think this dress is a good fit. Try another one. I am sure you will find a nicer dress."

Respect

Respect is one of the most important qualities in any relationship. Always respect your friends' thoughts, feelings, opinions, and time. You should also respect their privacy by protecting their secrets and never saying anything bad about them behind their backs.

Acceptance

You should never try to change your friends. Love and accept them as they are. Don't tell them how to dress, talk, act, etc., unless they ask for your opinion. The best gift you can give your friends is to let them be their unique and awesome selves around you.

Forgiveness

Forgive and forget is a great rule to live by, and it will make you very happy. Everyone makes mistakes.

You should let your friends know when they hurt or upset you. But once they explain themselves and say sorry, forgive them and follow Elsa's advice, "Let it go."

Don't keep bringing up their past mistakes every time you fight. Learn to forgive and forget.

Kindness

Always be kind to your friends.

- Meet them with a smile.
- When they do something wrong, listen to them with love and understanding instead of blaming them.
- Don't make fun of them or belittle their hopes and dreams.
- Thank them whenever they do something nice to you.

Peer Pressure

Peer pressure is when boys and girls your age influence you or make you do things you aren't comfortable with or don't want to do. For instance, your friends want to ditch school and go to the mall.

You tell them you don't want to and prefer to attend class instead. They tell you that you aren't cool or you are boring. So, you feel pressured to do as they say so they don't get mad at you. Then, you end up getting in trouble.

Setting Boundaries

You can resist peer pressure by setting boundaries.
https://www.pexels.com/photo/wood-garden-fence-board-48246/

You can resist peer pressure by setting boundaries. Boundaries are healthy rules you make to show your friends how you want to be treated. These rules are fair and make your life and relationships better and easier.

Decide your boundaries by sitting with yourself and thinking about the behaviors you can put up with and those that make you uncomfortable. You can even write them down.

When setting boundaries, you should only think about yourself and not other people's feelings. For instance, don't wonder whether this boundary will upset your friends or make them mad at you.

You aren't being selfish because your boundaries are meant to protect your mental health and make your life easier. They aren't hurting your friends.

Say "No" to anything that makes you uncomfortable. Actress Elizabeth Olsen once said, "No is a full sentence." You don't have to explain yourself or say why you don't want to do something. "No" is enough, and people should respect that without asking you, "Why?"

However, if you want to explain yourself to a friend, that's OK too. For instance, a friend asks you to help with her homework, but you have a big test tomorrow and haven't studied. You can tell her, "I can't. I am studying for an exam tomorrow and don't have the time." A good friend will be understanding and wish you good luck. She knows you care about her and would have helped her any other time.

However, a bad friend will make you feel guilty and even accuse you of being selfish when she is the one being a bad friend. In this case, if she pressures you, you must reply with a firm "No" without further explanation.

Make your boundaries clear to everyone in your life. If a friend crosses them once, give them a second chance. However, if they constantly step over your boundaries and make fun of you, you should ask yourself if this friendship is worth it.

Remember also to respect your friends' boundaries just like you want them to respect yours.

Having good friends is a beautiful gift. They give you love and support and are always there when needed. Take care of them and be an honest, accepting, and respectful friend.

Set boundaries to protect yourself from peer pressure and ensure everyone respects them.

Section 5: Hygiene and Self-Care Essentials

Growing up comes with a few changes to your hygiene routine, especially during puberty. This is when your body undergoes some significant changes, and it's essential to understand and manage them.

Good hygiene is not just about smelling nice or looking good.
https://www.pexels.com/photo/tray-with-bath-bomb-on-tub-6620948/

Good hygiene is not just about smelling nice or looking good. It's a big part of who you are as a person, and as you grow up, it becomes even more essential. When you were little, your parents probably cared for every aspect of your hygiene needs, like bathing, brushing your teeth, and combing your hair.

However, now that you're growing older, many changes are taking place. Puberty brings some exciting and not-so-exciting changes to your body. There's new hair, more sweat, oil production, growing parts, and even some new smells. It might sound like a lot to handle, but don't worry! With a little daily attention, you'll get a handle on your hygiene routine quickly.

Think about your favorite stuffed animal or plush toy. You love it, right? Now imagine if you never cleaned it or took care of it. Over time, it would get dirty, maybe even smelly, and not feel as huggable anymore. Your body is a bit like that beloved toy. It needs care and attention, too. When you shower regularly, brush your teeth, and keep yourself clean, it's a lot like giving your body a warm, fresh hug every day. You feel good, and people around you appreciate it too.

On the other hand, if you don't take care of your body, just like your stuffed animal, it can get a bit, well, not-so-huggable. You might feel uncomfortable, and others might notice too. That's why personal hygiene is so essential.

Exercising Regularly

Exercise isn't about trying to look like those picture-perfect models you see on Instagram. Those images are usually edited and unrealistic. Real beauty comes in all shapes and sizes, and it's about feeling good in your own skin. So, why is exercise so essential for you?

Real beauty comes in all shapes and sizes, and it's about feeling good in your own skin.
https://unsplash.com/photos/group-of-women-standing-on-rock-fragment-T6zu4jFhVwg

Well, it's not just about appearances. It's about keeping your body healthy and strong. Exercise is a friendly reminder to your body to keep moving. Just like a car needs to run to stay in good shape, your body needs to move to stay healthy.

Exercise isn't just about being "skinny" or adhering to society's unrealistic beauty standards. It's about being the best, healthiest version of yourself. When you exercise regularly, you're giving your body the tools it needs to stay fit and strong.

If you've ever felt breathless after climbing a set of stairs, you're not alone. That's your body telling you it's not used to the effort. However, if you make exercise a part of your routine, climbing stairs will be a piece of cake.

Plus, exercise isn't just about physical health. It's about mental health, too. When you move your body, your brain releases feel-good chemicals called endorphins. These little mood boosters can help you feel more confident, happier, and ready to take on the world!

Getting Proper Sleep

Life is full of exciting moments, and it might feel like you want to stay up late to finish that show or read one more chapter of your favorite book. It might seem like staying up late won't hurt, but getting enough sleep is crucial, especially for young girls.

When you don't get enough sleep, the effects show up quickly. You might feel super sleepy during class, cranky with your family, and tired throughout the day. Have you ever had trouble concentrating or staying focused in school? Sleep deprivation can make that happen. For example, imagine trying to solve a puzzle when you're really tired. It's much harder, right? That's because your brain needs sleep to recharge. Then you can be your best self during the day.

The long-term consequences of not getting enough sleep can be very dangerous. Lack of sleep can mess with your memory. You might forget important things, like where you left your homework or what you were supposed to tell your friend. Imagine how frustrating that can be!

Sleep deprivation can make your emotions go all over the place. You might find yourself getting upset or sad for no apparent reason. When you're sleep-deprived, your brain works more slowly. Long-term sleep problems can lead to serious health issues like obesity, heart problems, and even depression. Sleep deprivation can also make you more accident-prone. Think about it – if you're tired, you might not react as quickly if something unexpected happens.

So, here's the bottom line: sleep helps you be your best, feel your best, and stay safe. So, make sure to get the sleep you need each night – it's not just about feeling rested. It's about being your amazing self every day! So, put down that book or turn off the TV, and let yourself recharge with a good night's sleep. Your future self will thank you!

Eating Healthy

It's understandable. Eating junk food can be super fun. Who can resist a cup of ice cream or a juicy burger? While eating junk food occasionally is totally fine, it can become a problem if you do it too much. Junk food might taste great, but it often leaves you feeling tired and sluggish. You might notice that after eating a big fast-food meal, you feel like taking a long nap.

Eating junk food all the time can lead to health problems like obesity, heart disease, and diabetes. Too much junk food can even cause skin issues like acne. Healthy foods can help your skin look and feel its best.

Did you know that what you eat can affect your mood? Too much sugar or unhealthy fats can make you feel irritable or sad. Eating lots of junk food can give you tummy troubles. No one likes stomachaches, right?

So, here's the deal: it's okay to enjoy junk food occasionally, but the key is to find a balance. Make sure to fill your plate with lots of fruit, veggies, whole grains, and lean proteins. These foods will give you the energy and nutrients your growing body needs. Ask your parents to teach you which foods are good for you.

Skincare

Healthy skin can boost your confidence and make you feel great inside and out.
https://unsplash.com/photos/woman-in-white-tank-top-dPs0DEGrM9A

As you grow up, your body goes through some changes; many teens and tweens experience acne during this time. Acne is a common skin condition that often shows up during puberty. It happens when your hair follicles get clogged with oil and dead skin cells. Those little bumps and pimples you might see? Yep, that's acne. It's normal, and it happens to many people as their bodies grow and change.

Even if you don't have acne, taking care of your skin is super important. It helps keep your skin looking fresh, hydrated, and glowing. Who doesn't want that, right? Healthy skin can boost your confidence and make you feel great inside and out. So, here's a general skincare routine you can follow:

Morning Routine

- **Cleansing:** Start your day by washing your face gently with a mild, soap-free cleanser. This removes any dirt or sweat from overnight.

- **Moisturizing:** Apply a lightweight, non-comedogenic (won't clog pores) moisturizer to keep your skin hydrated.

- **Sun Protection:** If you're heading outside, use sunscreen with at least SPF 30 to protect your skin from the sun's harmful rays.

- **Night Routine**
- **Cleansing:** Before bedtime, cleanse your face to remove makeup, dirt, and oil. Make sure it's all gone!
- **Treatment:** If you have acne, use over-the-counter treatments with ingredients like benzoyl peroxide or salicylic acid. But follow the instructions and don't overdo it.
- **Moisturizing:** Apply your moisturizer once more to lock in hydration while you sleep.

Weekly Routine

- **Exfoliation:** Exfoliate your skin gently once a week to remove dead skin cells. Avoid scrubbing too hard to prevent irritation.
- **Face Masks:** Consider using a face mask once a week for an extra skin boost. Choose one that suits your skin type.

General Tips

- **Hands Off:** Try to resist touching your face throughout the day. Your hands can transfer dirt and bacteria to your skin.
- **Healthy Diet:** Eating a balanced diet with plenty of fruit and veggies helps your skin stay healthy.
- **Hydration:** Drink lots of water to keep your skin hydrated from the inside out.
- **Good Sleep:** Get enough sleep, as this is when your body repairs and rejuvenates your skin.

Remember, everyone's skin is unique. Be patient and gentle with your skincare routine. And here's some great advice: embrace your natural beauty, imperfections, and all. You're beautiful just the way you are and taking care of your skin is about feeling your best, inside and out.

Haircare

Taking care of your hair is more than just about looks. It's about keeping it healthy and strong. When your hair is well-cared for, it boosts your confidence and makes you feel your best. Plus, it's a major part of your overall self-care routine.

Curly Haircare:

Curly hair is absolutely stunning, but it often requires a bit more care to avoid frizz and maintain those beautiful curls.

- **Shampoo Less Often:** Curly hair tends to be drier, so you don't need to shampoo it every day. Try shampooing every few days or using a sulfate-free shampoo, which is gentler on curls.
- **Condition, Condition, Condition:** Use a good conditioner whenever you wash your hair. It helps keep your curls hydrated and reduces frizz.
- **Detangling:** Be gentle when detangling curly hair. Use a wide-tooth comb or your fingers when your hair is wet and coated with conditioner.
- **Avoid Heat:** Limit the use of heat-styling tools like flat irons or curling irons. Embrace your natural curls whenever possible to prevent damage.
- **Sleep on Silk:** Sleeping on a silk pillowcase reduces frizz and protects your curls while you snooze.

Straight Haircare:

Straight hair is equally beautiful and also needs some care to stay sleek and shiny.

- **Use a Mild Shampoo:** Opt for a mild, sulfate-free shampoo to keep your straight hair from becoming too dry.
- **Conditioner for Shine:** Apply conditioner to the ends of your hair for extra shine. Avoid applying it to your scalp, as it can make your hair look greasy.
- **Protect from Heat:** If you use heat styling tools, use a heat protectant spray to shield your hair from damage.
- **Trim Regularly:** Getting a trim every couple of months helps prevent split ends and keeps your straight hair looking neat.
- **Avoid Tight Hairstyles:** Wearing tight ponytails or braids frequently can damage your hair. Opt for loose styles whenever you can.

Remember, your hair is unique and beautiful, just the way it is. Embrace your natural texture and style and enjoy taking care of it as part of your self-care routine.

Nailcare

While getting acrylics and add-ons can look awesome, they can sometimes damage your nails. So, here's how you can care for your nails on your own.

DIY Manicure:

Doing your own manicure can be a lot of fun and a great way to keep your nails healthy. Here's how:

- **Clean and Trim:** Start by cleaning your nails with warm, soapy water. Gently push back your cuticles with a cuticle pusher or a wooden stick. Trim your nails evenly with a nail clipper.
- **File Carefully:** Use a nail file to shape your nails. Go for rounded or square shapes – whatever you like best!
- **Buff Smooth:** If you have a nail buffer, gently buff your nails to make them smooth. This step isn't necessary every time, but it can make your nails look extra nice.
- **Moisturize:** Apply a moisturizing hand cream to keep your hands and nails soft.
- **Polish or Not:** You can paint your nails with your favorite nail polish or leave them natural. If you do use polish, make sure to use a base coat to protect your nails.
- **Top It Off:** Finish with a clear topcoat to make your manicure last longer.

General Nail Care Tips:

- **Don't Bite:** Try your best to avoid biting your nails. It can damage them and isn't good for your teeth either!
- **Gentle on Glue:** If you love to wear stick-on nails, remove them gently. Soaking your nails in warm, soapy water can help loosen the glue.
- **Healthy Diet:** Eating a balanced diet with vitamins and minerals helps your nails stay strong.
- **Keep 'em Short:** Shorter nails are less likely to break, so consider keeping them trimmed.
- **Give 'em a Break:** If you love nail art, it's a good idea to let your nails breathe between manicures. Take a break from polish once in a while.

Remember, your nails are your canvas, and you can have lots of fun taking care of them and trying out different looks. So, keep it simple, keep it fun, and enjoy having beautiful, healthy nails!

Mental Health

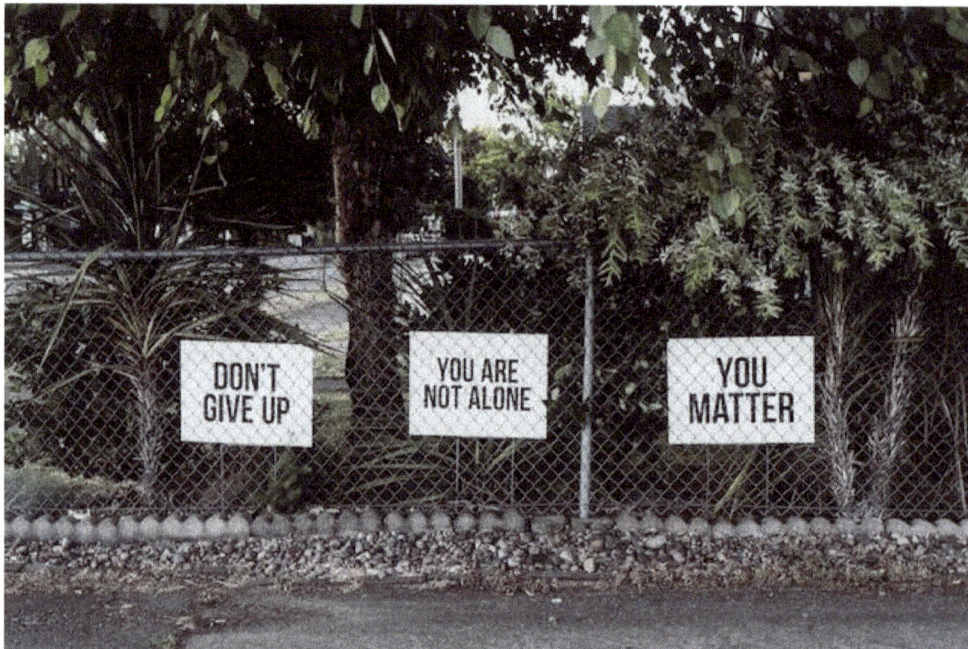

Remember that you're not alone when everything feels overwhelming.

Life can throw some challenging situations your way, and staying calm isn't always easy, especially during confrontations. These new years can be tough, but remember, you have the strength to make the best out of them. Remember that you're not alone when everything feels overwhelming, and you don't know where to turn. Many people care about you, and seeking help is a courageous step.

It's completely normal to feel stressed at times. At your age, you are dealing with difficult situations like:

- Academics
- Friendships
- Dating
- Fashion
- Negative influences
- Concerns about weight
- Bullying
- Family issues

Dealing with Common Issues

- **Anxiety:** Feeling anxious occasionally is normal. It might be due to new experiences, like entering middle school as a new student. Remember that adjusting takes time, and you will be fine.

- **Depression:** Leaving old friends behind can be difficult, but it doesn't mean you have to lose contact. Collect phone numbers, addresses, and email addresses and connect on social media. You have people who care about you no matter where you go.
- **Peer Pressure:** It's natural to want to fit in with your peers, but sometimes, you might feel pressure to do things you're uncomfortable with. It's perfectly OK to say no. You don't have to do anything that goes against your values or instincts.

In the journey of growing up, you'll face a range of emotions and challenges, but remember, you have the strength to overcome them. Reach out to the people who care about you, take care of your mental health, and always stay true to yourself.

Personal Hygiene

Sometime during the early stages of puberty, you or someone close to you might notice a new smell coming from your armpits. This is known as body odor, and it can be pretty strong in a not-so-great way. Handling body odor is easy. The solution is to wash your armpits every day with soap and water. So, no more just hanging out in the shower singing – you must raise your arm and soap under there! After you're clean and dry, apply deodorant to your pits.

The best time to apply deodorant is when you are clean and your pits are dry. If you shower or bathe at night, put your deodorant on at night. Some doctors believe applying it at night is more effective in reducing sweat the next day.

Another place that can develop funky smells during puberty is your feet. Have you ever noticed your mom putting your tennis shoes outside at night? That could be your first clue. Stinky feet are just another part of puberty. To keep your feet fresh, wash them with soap and water every day, and wear clean cotton socks or footies with closed-toe shoes. It also helps to avoid wearing the same pair of shoes every day.

Body Hair

In puberty, everyone eventually gets a visit from the "hairy fairy." You may notice new hairs in your armpits, darker hair on your legs, and, for some girls, darker hair on their face, especially the upper lip. All of this hair growth is entirely normal, and how much hair you grow can be influenced by your family background and where you live.

Whether you want to remove the hair depends on your preference. Girls with blond or light-colored hair might not feel the need to shave at all, while those with darker hair may choose to start earlier. You'll know it's time to start shaving when the hair bothers you or makes you self-conscious.

Hair Removal Methods
- **Shaving:** The most common method. Use your own razor and shaving cream. Be careful not to press too hard or shave dry skin to prevent irritation.
- **Creams (Depilatory Creams):** These dissolve hair. They are applied to the skin, let for a certain time, and then wiped away. Always test a small area of skin first to check for allergies or irritation.
- **Waxing:** This involves applying warm wax to the skin and quickly removing it along with the hair. Professionals often do it, but it can be done at home with adult supervision.

- **Other Hair Removal Methods:** Methods like laser or electrolysis are best done by professionals and can be expensive.

Facial Hair

Some girls may develop facial hair during puberty, especially in the upper lip area. You can lighten it with bleach or remove it using depilatory creams (for the face), waxing, or mini-electric razors made for facial use. Always be cautious when trying new methods on your face, and ask an adult for help.

Hygiene in Social Settings

When you're out and about in social settings, maintaining good hygiene is considerate and necessary for making a good impression. Here are some tips to help you stay fresh and confident:

- **Fresh Breath:** You'll want fresh breath when talking to friends, classmates, or new people. Brush your teeth regularly, use mouthwash, and carry sugar-free gum or mints for quick freshening up.
- **Clean Hands:** Shaking hands or giving high-fives is common in social situations. Keep your hands clean by washing them with soap and water. Consider carrying a small hand sanitizer for those times when a sink isn't available.
- **Public Restrooms:** When using public restrooms, remember to wash your hands thoroughly with soap and water before leaving. Use a paper towel to open the door if possible.
- **Perfume and Cologne:** While it's nice to smell good, be mindful not to overdo it with strong scents, as some people may be sensitive to fragrances.
- **Stay Fresh:** If you're planning a long day out, consider carrying a small hygiene kit with essentials like tissues, wet wipes, and a spare shirt, especially if you'll be active.
- **Period Hygiene:** Be prepared for your menstrual cycle by discreetly carrying sanitary pads or tampons in your bag and changing them regularly.

Be prepared for your menstrual cycle and choose your preferred menstrual product.
https://www.pexels.com/photo/pink-menstrual-cup-in-box-1560288/

Remember, good hygiene isn't just about appearances. It's also about taking care of your health and well-being. Proper hygiene ensures you're physically comfortable, which directly impacts your confidence. When you feel fresh and clean, you're more at ease in your own skin, and you'll engage with others confidently. Plus, taking care of your appearance by showering, grooming, and dressing well gives you positive feelings about yourself. When you like what you see in the mirror, your self-esteem gets a boost.

Section 6: Growth Mindset for Success

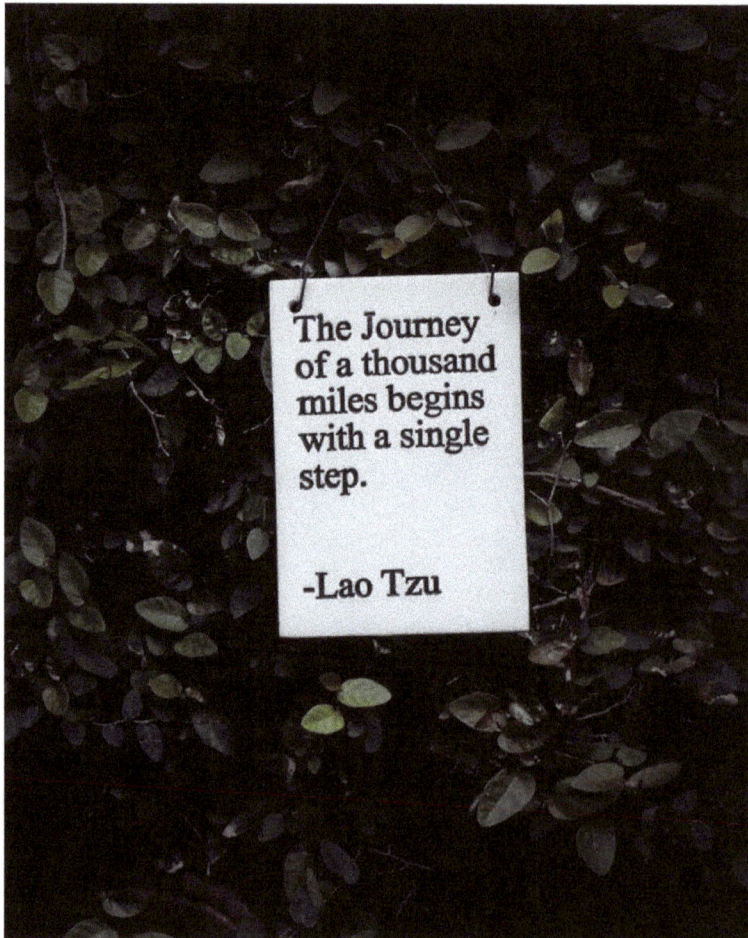

Your mindset is how you think and feel about yourself when faced with challenges.

Your mindset is how you think and feel about yourself when faced with challenges, learning new things, or trying something new. No one has entirely the same mindset and thoughts. Everyone's mindset is like a unique set of glasses that they wear to look at the world around them. Or think of it this way: your mindset is the engine that powers your thoughts and actions. It's how you see yourself, your abilities, and the world. There are two general types of mindsets in this world, which largely shape how you live your life. These include:

Fixed Mindset

Imagine you're trying to learn a new dance move and find it tricky. If you have a fixed mindset, you might think, "I can't do this; I'm just not a good dancer," and you might feel like giving up. In a fixed mindset, you believe your abilities are set in stone and can't change.

Growth Mindset

Now, with a growth mindset, you'd think, "This dance move is challenging, but I can learn it with practice and patience!" A growth mindset means you believe that, with effort and learning, you can become better at anything.

A growth mindset means you're open to learning. For instance, imagine you're learning to play the piano. With a growth mindset, you know that practicing will make you a better pianist. On the other hand, a fixed mindset will make you believe it is simply too hard for you to learn something so complex. Life sometimes throws challenges your way, but a growth mindset will help you bounce back from challenging situations. You won't give up easily because you believe in yourself and your ability to learn and overcome. For example, if you're trying to build a tall tower with blocks and it keeps falling, a growth mindset says, "I'll try a different way and keep building until it stands!"

When you dream big and set goals for yourself, a growth mindset keeps you on the path to success. You work hard because you know you can achieve your dreams. If you dream of becoming a scientist, a growth mindset inspires you to study, ask questions, and explore the world. Challenges become exciting adventures. You see them as opportunities to grow, not as scary obstacles. For instance, trying a new sport or recipe becomes a way to discover something new about yourself. Remember, having a growth mindset means believing in your power to improve and learn.

1. S.M.A.R.T. Goals

Goals help you stay focused, motivated, and excited about your dreams and the things you want to do. Setting goals is essential because goals help you know where you're headed and what steps you need to take to get there. Having goals gives you a reason to work hard and do your best. Achieving your goals makes you feel proud and confident in your abilities. Sometimes, you might face challenges when trying to reach your goals, and that's OK! It's a part of learning and growing.

Setting goals is like making a plan. Here's how to do it:

- First, think about what you want to achieve. It could be getting better at a sport, reading more books, or making new friends.
- Your goal should be easy to understand. Instead of saying, "I want to be a better reader," say, "I want to read one new book every month."
- Big goals can be a little overwhelming, so break them into smaller steps.

- Use the SMART Goals Technique:
  - **Specific:** Your goal should be clear and specific. Ask yourself: What exactly do I want to achieve?
  - **Measurable:** You should be able to track your progress. Ask yourself: How will I know when I've reached my goal?
  - **Achievable:** Your goal should be something you can realistically do. Ask yourself: Can I actually make this happen?
  - **Relevant:** Make sure your goal is important to you and makes sense in your life. Ask yourself: Why is this goal important to me?
  - **Time-Bound:** Set a deadline for your goal. Ask yourself: When do I want to achieve this?

2. **Decision-Making**

Every decision you make teaches you something new.
https://pixabay.com/photos/path-feet-shoes-road-surface-1610699/

Whether big or small, decisions are a part of life, and they're super important because they shape your future. Making decisions shows that you're responsible for your choices and actions. As you grow older, you will have to make more and more decisions for yourself, decisions your parents used to make. This responsibility will now fall on you, and you'll be in charge of your life story. Every decision you make teaches you something new, and good decisions boost your self-confidence because you feel capable and in control of your life. Here's how you can make good decisions:

- **Identify the Decision**

First, be clear about what decision you need to make. Sometimes, it helps to write it down or talk about it with someone you trust. Example: Imagine you're choosing whether or not to join a new school club that requires a lot of time and effort.

- **Gather Information**

Get all the facts you can about your options. Learn about the club, its activities, and what's expected of you. Research the club online, talk to current members, and ask your teacher about it.

- **List Pros and Cons**

Make a list of the good things (pros) and the not-so-good things (cons) about joining the club. This helps you see the benefits and drawbacks. Pros might include making new friends or learning new skills, while cons might involve the time commitment.

- **Consider Your Values**

Think about what matters most to you. Do the club's goals and activities match your interests and values? If you value spending time with your family after school, consider if joining the club will allow for that.

- **Ask for Advice**

Talk to people you trust, like your parents or friends, and ask for their opinions. They might have insights you haven't thought of. Ask your parents for their thoughts on how joining the club could fit into your schedule.

- **Visualize Outcomes**

Imagine what your life might look like with each decision. Picture how it could affect your daily routine, friendships, and happiness. Close your eyes and imagine a day in your life with the club and another day without it.

- **Make the Decision**

After considering all these factors, it's time to make your choice. Trust yourself and the research you've done. You decide to join the club because you're excited about the activities and you believe you can manage your time effectively.

No matter the outcome, every decision is a chance to learn and grow. If it turns out well, celebrate your success. If not, think about what you can do differently next time.

Learning from Failure

Learning from failure means turning mistakes into opportunities for growth. When things don't go as planned, it's a chance to figure out what went wrong and how to do better next time. This skill is needed whenever you try something new, face challenges, or make mistakes. It helps you become resilient, learn valuable lessons, and improve your abilities.

When you face a setback or make a mistake, take a moment to think about what you can learn from it. For example, if you didn't do well on a test, figure out which topics you need to study more and adjust your study routine accordingly. Ask yourself questions like, "What went wrong? What could I have done differently?" Then, think about how to apply what you've learned to improve next time. For instance, if you didn't do well on a science project, think about which parts were challenging and use that knowledge to improve your approach to the next project.

Time Management

Time management is the skill of using your time wisely.

Time management is the skill of using your time wisely. It means planning your activities and tasks to make the most of your day. You need time management when juggling schoolwork, hobbies, and other activities. It helps you stay organized, reduce stress, and have time for things you enjoy. Create a schedule or to-do list for your day. Break tasks into smaller steps. For instance, if you have homework and want to read a book, fit in time for both and stick to your schedule.

Critical-Thinking

Critical thinking is thinking deeply, analyzing information, and making thoughtful decisions. It's needed when solving puzzles, making choices, or understanding complex topics. It helps you make informed decisions and better understand the world around you. Practice thinking critically by asking questions. For example, when reading a news article, ask yourself, "Is this information reliable and trustworthy? Are there other perspectives to consider?"

Problem-Solving

Problem-solving is the skill of finding solutions to challenges or puzzles. It's needed when facing difficulties in schoolwork, conflicts with friends, or everyday life situations. It helps you overcome obstacles, make decisions, and achieve your goals. Start with simple problems. For example, if you're trying to fit all your toys into a box, experiment with different ways to arrange them until they all fit. Gradually, you'll get better at finding solutions to more complex problems.

Effort and Persistence

Effort and persistence mean working hard and not giving up, even when things are challenging. It's useful for learning new skills, facing tough situations, or pursuing long-term goals. It helps you achieve your dreams and build confidence in your abilities. Set a goal and work towards it, even when it gets tough. For instance, if you're learning a new instrument, practice regularly, even when you find it hard. Over time, you'll improve.

Study and Research

Study and research involve learning new information, exploring topics, and discovering new things. This helps with school projects, understanding the world, and pursuing your interests. You'll excel in school, satisfy your curiosity, and become more knowledgeable. When you're curious about a topic, like space or animals, visit the library or use the internet to find books, articles, or videos about it. Take notes and share what you've learned with friends or family.

Positive Self-Talk

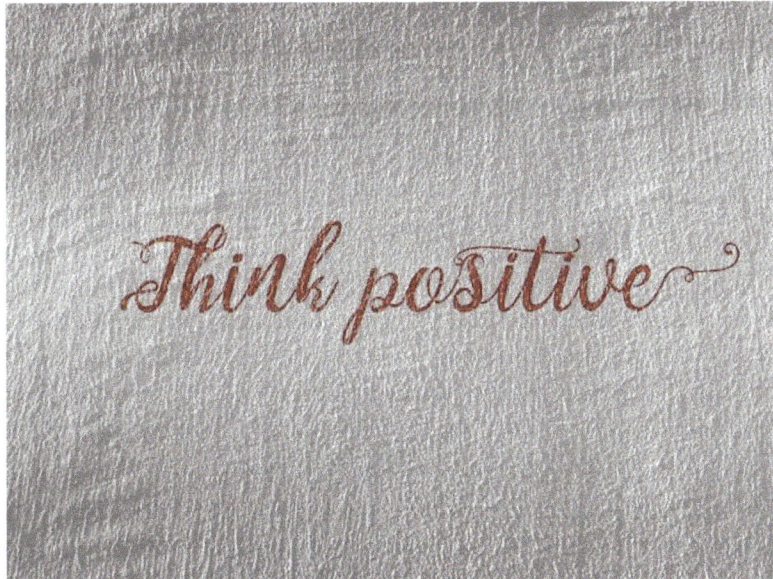

Positive self-talk is about being kind to yourself and using encouraging words when facing setbacks.
https://unsplash.com/photos/think-positive-text-illustration-qe5mRoPJjQ0

Positive self-talk is about being kind to yourself and using encouraging words when facing setbacks. Use positive self-talk when you're feeling discouraged, nervous, or unsure of yourself. It boosts your confidence, reduces anxiety, and helps you stay motivated. Imagine you're trying a new sport, and you make a mistake. Instead of saying, "I'm terrible at this," tell yourself, "It's OK, I'm learning, and I'll get better with practice." Encourage yourself like you would a friend. For instance,

- **Negative Thought:** "I'm not good at this."

Positive Self-Talk: "I can get better with practice."

- **Negative Thought:** "I don't have any friends."

Positive Self-Talk: "I can make new friends by being kind."

- **Negative Thought:** "I'm so confused."

Positive Self-Talk: "I can learn and understand this over time."

- **Negative Thought:** "I look yucky today."

Positive Self-Talk: "I look great just the way I am."

- **Negative Thought:** "I can't do it."

Positive Self-Talk: "I can do it if I try my best."

- **Negative Thought:** "I'm always making mistakes."

Positive Self-Talk: "Mistakes help me learn and grow."

- **Negative Thought:** "Nobody likes me."

Positive Self-Talk: "I'm a good friend, and I can make more friends."

- **Negative Thought:** "I'm too scared to try."

Positive Self-Talk: "I can be brave and try new things."

- **Negative Thought:** "I'll never be as good as her."

Positive Self-Talk: "I'm special in my own way."

- **Negative Thought:** "I'm a failure."

Positive Self-Talk: "I can learn from my mistakes and succeed."

Adaptability

Adaptability is the skill of adjusting to new situations and being flexible when things change. It's needed when plans don't go as expected or when you face unexpected challenges. It helps you handle unexpected events, stay calm, and find creative solutions. Try new things and embrace change. For example, if a rainy day changes your outdoor plans, adapt by finding an indoor activity like drawing or playing a board game.

With a growth mindset, you can accomplish anything you set your heart and mind to. Don't shy away from challenges; seek them out. They are your chance to shine and grow. Remember, it's OK to struggle because that's how you learn and become stronger. Make curiosity your best friend. Be curious about the world around you, ask questions, and seek answers. And remember to not only celebrate your achievements but also the hard work and effort you put into everything you do. Every small step you take is a victory on your journey. Finally, keep your self-talk positive and supportive. Encourage yourself when things get tough, and remember that mistakes are stepping stones to success. Life is a once-lived adventure filled with endless opportunities for growth and learning. The skills you're developing today will help you tomorrow. So, embrace every moment, stay curious, and believe in yourself with steady confidence.

Section 7: Being Confident

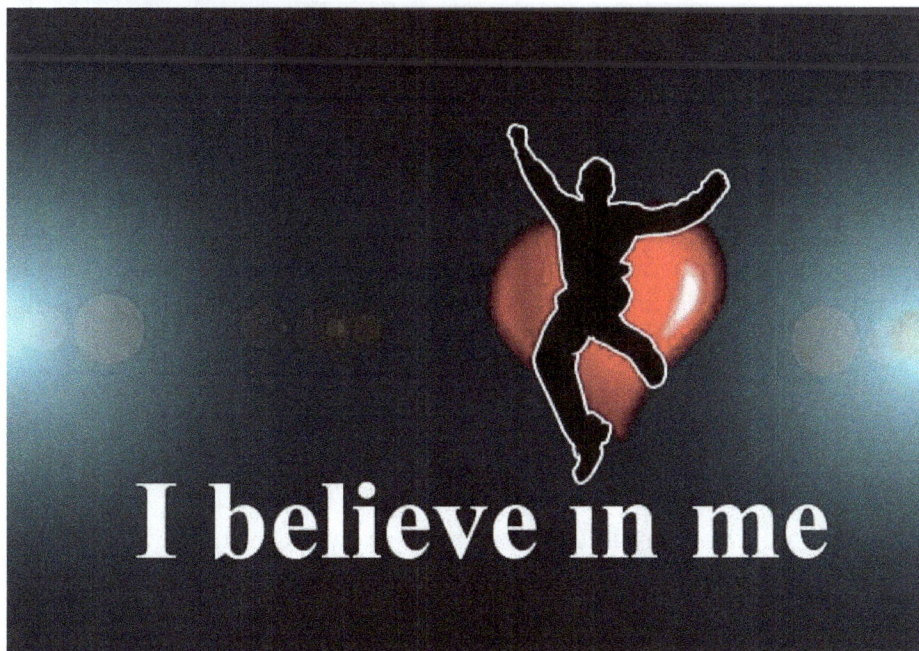

Self-confidence is among the traits that most successful people have.
https://pixabay.com/illustrations/heart-self-esteem-self-liberation-741502/

Self-confidence is among the traits that most successful people have. Successful individuals believe in themselves and their abilities, which allows them to achieve whatever they put their minds to. In this section, you will understand confidence and why it's important. You'll learn about the different types of confidence and how each can improve different aspects of your life. You will also find several tips and strategies, such as practicing positive self-talk and developing presentation skills, to help you become more confident.

What Is Self-Confidence?

Has anyone ever complimented your personality? Perhaps they told you you were really creative, good at art, or excellent at your sport. How did that make you feel about yourself? Did this boost your confidence, or did you doubt all the good things they said about you? Questioning whether what they said about you is true is the opposite of self-assurance and confidence.

Being confident means that you believe you're capable and worthy of receiving compliments. Feeling sure of your skills and abilities is the best way to achieve your goals. You won't be motivated to study if you don't believe in your ability to do well in your tests. You might tell yourself, "It doesn't matter if I study hard. I won't get the full grade anyway." If you're confident, on the other hand, you'll truly believe that you'll get the full grade if you study hard enough. This will motivate you to study hard and actually get the highest score. Having self-confidence is the key to working toward your goals without giving up.

One of the best qualities of self-assured people is that they don't need external validation. This means they don't need others always to compliment and reassure them that they're skilled and talented to feel good about themselves. Everyone wants others to appreciate their abilities from time to time. However, you can't rely on other people's compliments to know that you're amazing the way you are.

The Importance of Confidence

Many people mistake confidence for arrogance and hesitate to believe in themselves and their abilities. Those who are truly self-confident don't feel better than others. Instead, they don't compare themselves to anyone because they're sure of their capabilities.

While everyone sometimes feels worried and overwhelmed, confident people are less likely to feel anxious or troubled when everyday challenges arise. They know that they can handle anything that comes their way. Self-assured individuals don't pay much attention to people's opinions. They know that doing their best and thinking and feeling positively about themselves is all that matters. Most importantly, they have an "I can" rather than an "I can't" mindset.

Confidence allows you to take on life's new experiences and opportunities bravely. You are more likely to welcome positive changes into your life, meet new people, try new things, and develop when you realize your capabilities. Instead of beating yourself up and feeling discouraged when things don't go your way, self-assurance makes you ready to try again.

People with low self-confidence aren't as open to self-growth as others. They're hesitant to try new things and explore new opportunities. If they fail at something, they will probably not try it again, even if it is their first time doing it. It's normal to fail at new things a couple of times before you start getting the hang of them. It's also very common to feel afraid of messing things up. However, you shouldn't let these worries and your lack of self-assurance hold you back from working toward your dreams and goals.

Types of Confidence

Task-Specific Confidence

This type of confidence means that you believe in your ability to complete a certain task. When you're confident you can do something well, you'll feel excited to learn more and grow your skillset. You'll want to challenge yourself and won't be afraid of trying. For example, if you're confident in your reading skills, you will likely excel in English class. You might also challenge yourself to read and understand books above your grade level.

General Confidence

People with this type of confidence believe in their abilities in different parts of life. They are not just confident about one of their skills, but they fully trust in themselves. Being generally confident improves your self-esteem or the way you think about yourself. It makes you more willing to take on new challenges and go on new journeys with a positive "I can do it" attitude. Generally confident people make new friends easily, try out new activities and sports, thrive in group work, and participate in public speaking activities or class discussions. They don't hesitate to speak up and share their opinions and ideas because they know their thoughts and views are valuable.

Situational Confidence

Situational confidence is when you feel confident in certain situations or environments. Practicing situational confidence makes you feel comfortable, and you will easily socialize in new social situations. You might be able to handle conflicts and arguments or speak and act confidently, even when nervous.

How to Be More Confident

Engage In Positive Self-Talk

Did you know that your brain believes whatever you repeat? If you always tell yourself you're not skilled or talented, you will feel really bad about yourself. Say you took up tennis, but tell yourself you're not good at it. Every time you go to your tennis session, you'll feel down and worry about missing your shots. Whenever you're about to shoot the ball, you think, "I'm really bad at this. I'm probably going to miss this shot, too." Your negative thoughts and feelings distract you while playing, which causes you to actually miss.

Talking to yourself positively, on the other hand, leads to positive results. You'll be more enthusiastic if you constantly tell yourself that you're great for your level and you're getting better with each session you take. You'll genuinely believe that you're capable of making all the shots and won't have any negative thoughts distracting you. Approaching situations with positive emotions helps you learn better and improve your skills.

Interrupt all negative thoughts about yourself and change them into something more positive. For instance, if the thought "I can't make the shot" is racing through your mind, interrupt and replace it with "I can make it if I put my mind to it."

Repeat Positive Affirmations

Since your mind believes everything you repeat, you can benefit from repeating positive affirmations. Positive affirmations are kind and uplifting sentences that you can repeat to yourself over and over to feel happier, stronger, and more confident. Repeating these statements until your mind believes them will help you believe in yourself.

Here are a few positive affirmations to boost your confidence:

- I am enough.
- I believe in myself.
- I have valuable skills and talents.
- I am capable of making amazing things happen.
- I am proud of my achievements.
- I am always getting closer to my goals.

You can create your own positive affirmations for any purpose you want. The statements should start with "I," be in the present tense ("am" or "have" instead of "was" or "will"), and, of course, be inspiring and positive.

I

I

I

I

I

I

I

I

Don't Compare Yourself to Others

Everyone compares themselves to others from time to time. It's normal to catch yourself thinking, "I wish I were smart like James," or "Why can't I be as artistic as Sophia?" Sometimes, thinking about other people's qualities can encourage you to develop the traits you admire. However, more often than not, it leaves you feeling bad and thinking negatively about yourself. Whenever you compare yourself to others, remember that everyone has unique qualities and skills. Life would be pretty boring if everyone were exactly the same, right?

Identify and Focus on Your Talents

Think about all the things you're good at instead of focusing on what you don't have.

Just as you admire other people's qualities, you have traits and skills that others wish they had. Think about all the things you're good at instead of focusing on what you don't have. Do you play a sport or an instrument? Not everyone in the world knows how to play your sport or instrument. Do you draw or paint? Many people can easily doodle a smiley face, but not everyone can draw and paint beautiful landscapes and portraits. Are you an excellent listener? This is an important skill that many people lack. It makes others feel heard and understood. Write down all your good qualities and skills on a piece of paper. Focus on how you can improve them and shine instead of dwelling on the qualities you don't have.

Practice Self-Acceptance

Confidence has nothing to do with looks as it comes from within. Even the best-looking people may not be confident if they let their insecurities get in the way. Insecurities are physical, personality-related, or skill-related things people are unsure about. Many of the most talented people care deeply about what others think, which makes them less confident.

To be confident, you must accept yourself as you are. Every morning, think about all the things you love about yourself and remember that everyone has imperfections. Not everything you see on TV or social media is real. Many specialized apps and editing programs make celebrities and influencers seem perfect – *when no one is.* Aside from looks, the incredible lifestyles you see online aren't necessarily true either.

What you see on TV and social media is a small part of the real story. People naturally want to show off the best aspects of their lives, tricking you into believing they're always happy. When you compare yourself to others online, remember that most of what you see isn't real.

Learn to Take Constructive Criticism Gracefully

When handled correctly, constructive criticism can be valuable for personal growth and development. Constructive criticism is feedback meant to help you do things more effectively. Having someone point out your flaws and mistakes can sting, which is why you need to learn to respond to them and accept them with an open mind.

You might feel the need to cry or lash out when someone criticizes you. However, the first step in dealing with feedback is to stay calm and avoid reacting right away. Don't cut people off and give them the chance to speak. Listen carefully and understand what they're saying and why they're saying it. When you feel angry, remember the benefits of accepting feedback that will help you do better in the future. Simply thank the person for their opinion, regardless of whether you agree or disagree with them.

Improve Your Public Speaking and Presentation Skills

- **Speak Clearly**

Rehearse your speeches, arguments, and presentations beforehand. Make sure that you're speaking at a reasonable volume. Your voice shouldn't be too low that people can't hear you, nor too loud that it's annoying to listen to. Maintain an average speed of speaking. You shouldn't be too slow, boring, fast, or hard to understand. Research words you don't know how and learn how to pronounce them to ensure you're understood.

- **Look at a Friend**

If you feel nervous, search for a friend or any familiar face in the crowd. Look at them and pretend that you're having a conversation with them. This will help you feel more comfortable and less anxious. Once you feel more confident, look around the room.

- **Pay Attention to Your Body Language**

Having a slouched back or crossed arms can make you seem insecure. Remember to stand up straight throughout the presentation. Don't tense your shoulder muscles. Keep them relaxed because this will help you breathe more easily. Keep your feet still, and don't move around too much. Avoid actions that show you're nervous, such as fiddling with your fingers and twirling your hair.

Confidence is among the most important skills anyone can have. It helps you tackle challenges, make new friends, and gain fascinating experiences. Confident individuals don't need others to reassure and compliment them constantly. They are aware of their capabilities and don't care deeply about the opinions of others.

Section 8: Money Matters

Have you ever had your heart set on something? Maybe you saw a sparkling new bicycle on your way back from school, a fluffy pet bunny in the pet store, or you really want tickets to see your favorite band in concert. You can almost see it, touch it, and feel the excitement welling up inside you. You might even be thinking about all the fun you'll have with the stuff you get. But wait! The first step to getting this stuff is to have enough money. Money is something that can turn those dreams into reality. It's not just pieces of paper or shiny coins. It's the key to making things happen.

Money is something that can turn those dreams into reality.

So, why is learning about money and how to manage it a big deal? Well, as you grow older, you'll discover that money is like a friendly guide, helping you along the path of life. Whether you want to buy the coolest gadgets, explore exciting places, or help others, knowing how to handle money is a skill you'll need more and more. For instance, maybe you and your friends decide to go to a theme park. It's a day filled with laughter and unforgettable memories. However, if you don't make a plan for your money, you might find yourself missing out on ice cream or not having enough tokens for games.

Or consider this: you've been saving up for your dream treehouse in the backyard. It's a cozy hideaway, perfect for reading, dreaming, and stargazing. But if you don't know how to manage your money wisely, you might be waiting longer than you'd like to see your treehouse dreams come true. Or, if you think about it in the long term, imagine you're all grown up and in charge of your own money. You're shopping for clothes, picking out cool phones, and saving for bigger goals like college or your own place to live. This is where money management will be super helpful for you.

If you don't know how to manage your money properly, it won't matter if you earn a lot. You'll still be left empty-handed at the end of the day. That is where this chapter comes in! It will teach you the secrets of managing your money, setting goals, and achieving your dreams.

Understanding Money

Think of money as the "universal language" everyone understands. When you have money, you can exchange it for toys, books, ice cream – or even save it for later. Money buys you things you like, just like how you trade your favorite stickers with friends. It can be a piece of paper with special marks on it, like numbers and pictures. You'll see these papers with the names of countries on them, like dollars, euros, or yen. People agree that these papers have value, so you can use them to get stuff.

Money isn't just paper and coins. It can also be numbers on a screen, just like in video games. These days, there is something called "digital money." It's the money you see in the bank, on your computer, or your parent's phone. It's a way to keep track of how much money you have without needing to carry coins or bills. For example, imagine you have an online piggy bank. You can see how much money you have saved right on your computer or tablet. It's like magic, right? This digital money can be used to buy things online or even in a store if they accept it. For example:

- When you buy your favorite ice cream with money you earned from chores or allowance, you are using paper money.
- If your parents send you some money as a gift on your birthday using a mobile app, that's digital money.
- When you drop a coin into a charity box to help others, that's also money!

So, whether it's coins jingling in your pocket, paper bills in your piggy bank, or numbers on a screen, they all represent money. And this is your ticket to make your dreams come true, one dollar at a time! And the more you understand about money, the better you'll be at turning those dreams into reality.

Where Money Comes From

Money, like a treasure, comes from different places. Some of it is handed to you as an allowance, a special gift, or even earned through small jobs.

1. **Allowances**

An allowance is money your parents or guardians give you regularly. It's a way for them to help you learn about money. Let's say you receive $5 from your parents weekly as an allowance. They might give it to you for doing your chores, being responsible, or just because they want you to learn about money. With your allowance, you can learn how to budget, save, or even treat yourself to a small toy or a tasty snack. For instance, your parents might give you $5 weekly to save up for that cool art set you've been wanting.

2. Gifts

Gifts can be in the form of money given to you on your birthday, during holidays, or for special achievements like getting good grades. Relatives and friends often give gifts to celebrate special moments in your life. When you receive money as a gift, you can save it for something big or use it to buy a fun treat. For instance, your grandparents may give you $10 on your birthday, which you can save to buy a new book or toy.

3. Potential Sources of Income

There are many ways to earn money beyond allowances and gifts. For example, you can help with chores around the house or even babysit for a neighbor. When you do these tasks, you're providing a service, and in return, you earn money. It's your first job! For instance, maybe you earned $2 for helping with the dishes or $10 for babysitting your neighbor's pet. These earnings can be added to your savings or used for something you really want. Some more ways you can earn extra money are:

- Helping with chores around the house (like setting the table or folding laundry).
- Offering to water your neighbor's plants when they're away.
- Selling lemonade or homemade crafts (like friendship bracelets) to neighbors or at a local market.

Remember, the money you earn, whether it's from your allowance, gifts, or doing small jobs, is your tool for making your dreams come true. By learning how to manage it wisely, you can have fun now and save for bigger adventures in the future.

Setting Financial Goals

Financial goals are dreams with a plan.
https://unsplash.com/photos/person-writing-on-brown-wooden-table-near-white-ceramic-mug-s9CC2SKySJM

Financial goals are dreams with a plan. They're the things you really want, and you're creating a special plan to make them happen. These goals can be small, like buying your favorite book or a toy you've had your eye on, or they can be big, like saving for something in the future, maybe for a family trip or even your college education. For instance, your financial goal might be to save $50 to buy that amazing art set you've been dreaming about. Or it could be to save $200 to go on a fun adventure with your family during the summer vacation. Whatever it is, it's something that makes you really happy, and you're making a plan to get there.

Why Setting Goals Is Important

Setting goals gives purpose to your money. It helps you make smart choices about how to use it. Think about it like this: Imagine you really, really want something special, like a new bicycle with a basket to carry your favorite books. If you set a goal to save your allowance or money from chores to buy that bicycle, you'll soon make your wish come true. For example, your goal might be to save $50 for the bicycle. You're one step closer to your goal every time you put money into your savings jar.

Set Achievable Goals

Sometimes, it's helpful to have short-term goals (things you want soon) and long-term goals (things you want in the future). Short-term goals include buying a new book or getting a small toy. Long-term goals are bigger, like saving for a big family trip or even for college when you grow up. You must prioritize your goals. This means deciding which ones are most important. For example, if you want a new book and want to save for a pet bunny, you can decide which one to focus on first. Your short-term goal could be to save $10 for a new book you want. Your long-term goal might be to save $200 for a family trip to the beach next summer.

Tracking Progress towards Goals

Make a checklist for your dreams. You can keep a special notebook where you write down your goals and how much money you've saved. Seeing your progress is fun because it shows you're getting closer to what you want. For instance, you can create a goal page for your new book in your notebook. Write down how much you need to save, and every time you save a bit, add it to your goal page. This way, you can see how close you are to getting your book.

The Value of Saving

Saving money is like planting seeds for your future. Imagine a sunny day when everything is perfect, and you're playing at the park. But then, it starts raining out of nowhere, and you get wet. If you have an umbrella (which you bought with saved money), you'll stay dry and happy, even on rainy days. So, why is saving important? It's being prepared with an umbrella for life. You save money for those unexpected rainy days. It can be for fun, a new toy, or something big like a college fund. Saving gives you the power to prepare for the future, no matter what surprises it brings. Think of saving as collecting shiny coins in a piggy bank. When your piggy bank is full, you can use that money to buy a special treat or save it for something amazing, like a cool science kit.

Delayed Gratification

Delayed gratification means having the patience and discipline to wait for something you want instead of spending your money on something small right now. It's choosing between a quick, tasty cookie or a whole, delicious cake you need to bake and wait for. When you practice delayed gratification, you're becoming a money wizard. You're learning that good things are worth waiting for, like saving up for that fantastic treehouse you've been dreaming about instead of spending all your money on candy today.

Imagine you have $10, and there's a new video game you want to buy for $15. If you buy candy with that $10 now, you'll have a lot of sweets for a short time, but you won't be any closer to your video game. However, if you save that $10 and add more to it later, you'll have enough to buy and enjoy the game for a long time.

1. **Patience and Discipline**

Imagine seeing a super-duper, extra delicious ice cream sundae with all your favorite toppings at a carnival. You have some money in your pocket and can buy it right now. But you remember that you have a bigger plan – you want to save for a trip to the theme park with your friends next month. Delayed gratification means you have the patience to say, "I'll pass on that ice cream today because I have a bigger adventure in mind for the future." It's about waiting and being OK with not having something immediately. For instance, you might really want that ice cream, but you choose to save your money for the theme park trip with your friends. It's tough to wait, but you know the fun at the theme park will be even sweeter!

2. **Trade-Offs (Spending Now vs. Saving for Something Bigger)**

Imagine you have $20. You can spend it all on small treats now, like candies and stickers, or you can save it for something bigger, like a new bicycle you've been dreaming about. It's like choosing between a handful of seashells or waiting a bit longer to collect beautiful pearls. Delayed gratification teaches you about trade-offs. It's making decisions about what's more important to you right now. It's deciding whether you want a few small joys today or a big, incredible adventure tomorrow. For example, you have $20 and really want those small treats. But you can buy a bicycle if you wait and save a little more. You choose to trade the small joys now for the fantastic adventure waiting for you in the future.

Creating a Simple Budget

A budget is a special plan for your money. It keeps track of how much money you have and where it goes. It's like having a map for your financial journey. With a budget, you make your money work for you in the best way possible.

Components of a Budget

Income (Allowances, Gifts, Potential Sources): This is money you receive. It's like the *money rain* that falls into your piggy bank. Your income can come from different places, like your weekly allowance, birthday gifts, or money you earn from doing chores. **For Example:** Let's say your weekly allowance is $10, and your grandma gave you $20 for your birthday. That's $30 in total as your income.

Expenses (Essential vs. Optional): Expenses are things you spend your money on. Some expenses are essential, like groceries or school supplies, while others are optional, like buying toys or going out for ice cream. For Example, You might spend $5 on a new notebook for school (essential) and $10 on a cool new art set (optional).

Savings (Allocating a Portion of Income): Savings are the treasure chest you're building for your dreams. It's the money you set aside for special goals or for the future. It's super important to save a part of your income to make your dreams come true.

Creating a Basic Budget

Let's say your weekly allowance is $10. You decide to save $3, spend $5 on a fun trip to the library with your friends, and put $2 in a jar to save for a special art kit. Your budget helps you see where every dollar goes.

Your budget might look like this:
- Savings: $3.
- Library fun with friends: $5.

- Special art kit savings: $2.
- Total: $10.

Budgeting Tools

To make budgeting even easier, you can use special tools. It's the same as having a handy map while you explore new places. You can use simple worksheets or apps on your computer or smartphone to track your money. These tools help you see how much you have, where you spend it, and how much you save. You can use a budget worksheet that your parents help you set up. It's a chart where you write down your income, your expenses, and how much you save. Or you can use a child-friendly budgeting app that makes it even more fun to manage your money.

Monthly Budget

Income Source	AMOUNT
TOTAL :	

NOTES

FIXED EXPENSES	BUDGET	SPENT
TOTAL :		

VARIABLE EXPENSES	BUDGET	SPENT
TOTAL :		

SAVING FOR?	SAVED
TOTAL SAVED :	

DEBT	PAID
TOTAL PAID :	

_____ - _____ = _____
TOTAL BUDGET   TOTAL SPENT

Learning about money isn't just about coins and dollars. It's about having the power to shape your future, to turn your dreams into reality. It's about being in control and making smart choices. As you grow older, these skills become even more necessary. Money isn't just about buying toys or treats. It's about achieving your goals, whether it's attending your dream college, traveling the world, or creating the most fantastic treehouse in the neighborhood. Moreover, understanding money teaches you to be a thoughtful decision-maker. It's about practicing patience and discipline, learning to wait for something bigger and better. It's the ability to make choices that bring bigger rewards in the future.

Section 9: Household Tasks

You have probably read the title of this section and thought, "Oh no, household tasks, really?" Yes, no one likes to do chores, and honestly, robot servants can't come soon enough, right? However, until they develop this technology, you will need to learn to do these things for yourself.

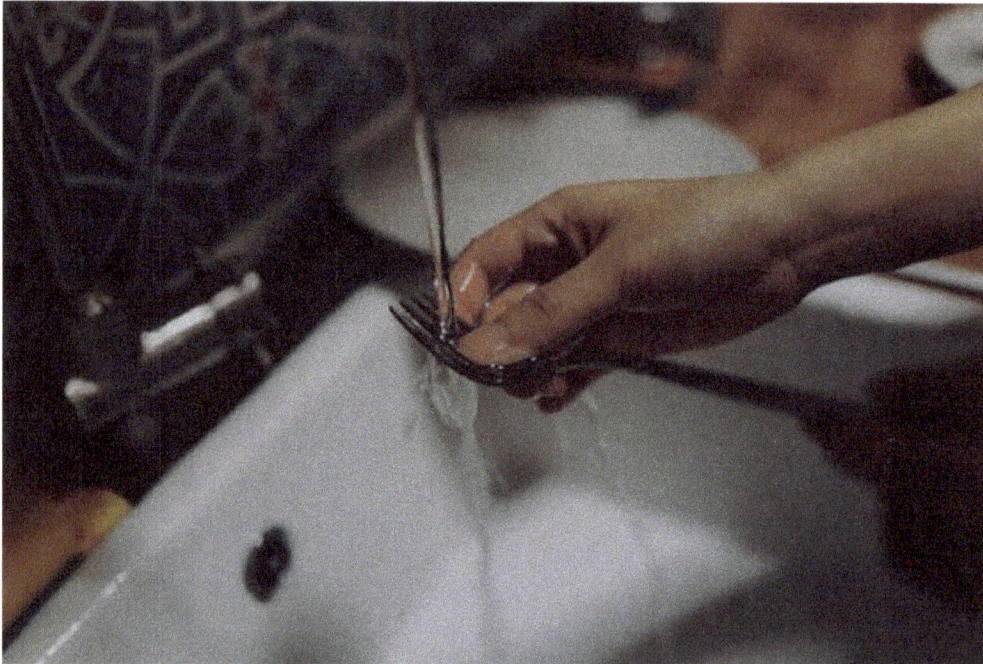

Doing chores doesn't have to be boring.

Doing chores doesn't have to be boring. You can make anything fun by turning on music – or even singing and dancing while vacuuming or setting the table! Who said life can't be a musical?

Are you ready to discover household tasks that can teach you to become more independent, responsible, and capable?

The Importance of Household Tasks

Why do your parents keep telling you to do your chores? You probably think, "Chores are boring, and I am too young for this type of responsibility." However, your parents don't do this to annoy you. They know that learning to do these tasks from an early age will benefit you now and in the future.

You may wonder, "What can I learn from sweeping the floor or preparing a meal?" These tasks make you capable and independent. You can do these things yourself rather than waiting for your mom to make dinner or clean your room.

When you (and your siblings) help your parents with household tasks, you become part of a team. Doing chores will also make you feel accomplished as you help out around the house. You will also learn essential skills to care for yourself when growing up.

Being an adult isn't always easier, and your parents are busier than you think. They have many things to take care of, like their jobs, home, errands, household tasks, and family. It would be nice to help out and make things easier for them. When everyone at home works together, the chores will finish faster, and you will all have free time to spend together as a family and have fun.

Since your parents don't always have time to finish all the chores, this can affect your home. There will be many dishes in the sink, dust on the furniture and the floor, and a mess all around the house. When you do your chores, you aren't just helping your parents; you are also ensuring that your home is always clean and organized for your and your family's sake.

Basic Cleaning Tasks

Now that you understand why you should do your household tasks, you are ready to learn about the chores that lie ahead.

The first thing you should learn about is basic cleaning, which includes removing dust and dirt from the house using different methods. Don't worry, this is easier than you think.

Dusting

Dusting doesn't only keep your home clean. It also protects you and your family from allergies and illnesses like sneezing, eye irritation, and coughing.

Instructions:

1. Remove everything from the top of furniture, like statues or photo frames.
2. Using a dusting cloth, wipe the dust off the furniture.
3. Get another piece of cloth and dust all the items you removed off the furniture before returning them.

Safety Tips

- If you are allergic to dust or it causes you breathing irritation, wear a face mask before you start.
- If dust hurts your eyes or makes them itchy, wear goggles.
- Always wear gloves while dusting.

Sweeping

Sweeping improves the air quality in your home and protects you and your family against allergies, runny nose, and watery eyes. It also keeps your floor clean so you and your siblings can run around the house without the risk of tripping on something and falling.

Wear a mask or goggles if the dust irritates you.

Instructions:

1. Choose a broom that you feel comfortable working with and holding.

Find a spot in the room to start sweeping from. Some people prefer to start at the edges, while others start at one end of the room. There is no right or wrong answer. Just choose whatever makes you comfortable.

2. Start sweeping all the dirt into a pile, then sweep the pile into a dustpan.
3. Slowly and carefully dump the dust pile into the trash.
4. Wash your hands after you finish.

Mopping

After you finish sweeping the floor, you should start mopping. Mopping removes germs from the floor, keeps it clean and sanitized, and reduces allergies.

Instructions:

1. Fill a bucket with water, then add a detergent. Read the instructions on the detergent to know how much soap to add to the water.
2. Dip the mop into the bucket for a few seconds, then get it out.
3. Wring the mop out as it should be damp, not wet, or it will damage the floor.
4. Start mopping the floor in a straight line.
5. For sticky spots, apply pressure with the mop and rub the area back and forth.
6. After mopping the whole area, fill another bucket with water and rinse the floor with the mop.
7. Leave the floor to dry.

Safety Tips

- Wear gloves at all times, and don't touch the detergent.
- Wash your hands very well after you finish.

Vacuuming

Vacuuming removes the dust from carpets, improves air quality, and protects against allergies.

Wear a face mask if the dust irritates you.

Instructions:

1. Check the vacuum bag. If it's half full or more, empty it or replace it.
2. Start vacuuming every part of your house, like the curtains, furniture, and floor. It's best to start with the curtains and end with the floor. Use the soft brush attachments for drapes and furniture.
3. When cleaning the carpets, you may need to go over the same spot more than once to remove the dust between the fibers.

Laundry Basics

Congratulations, you have cleaned your house and are ready to wash your clothes. Doing laundry removes fleas, dirt, and bacteria from your clothes that can cause infection or irritation.

Instructions for Doing Laundry:

1. Read the label on your clothes to know whether they're machine-washable – and if you should wash them in warm or cold water. Instructions differ for each fabric, so always read the label, or you will risk ruining your clothes. (The label looks similar to the picture below).

Read the label on your clothes.

2. Place clothes labeled "hand washed" and "washed separately" into different piles. You will also find clothes labeled "dry clean only." Put them in a bag for your parents to take to the dry cleaner.

3. Next, sort your laundry by color. Put white background prints, light grays, pastels, and whites on one pile. Dark-colored clothes like dark gray, brown, navy blue, red, and black should go in another pile.

4. Sort the two piles, but this time by fabric. For instance, your jeans and blouses should be in separate piles.

5. Read the instructions on the detergent before using it, then add it to the washer dispenser (the part that resembles a drawer in the washing machine).

6. Choose the best cycle for the fabric in the machine. Most fabrics are washed in a normal cycle. However, some will need a heavy-duty cycle, like towels and jeans. Only bedsheets, towels, and cotton underwear should be washed in hot water. The rest should be washed in cold water.

7. Before putting the clothes in the washing machine, check that the pockets are empty; one of your family members might have left a tissue, a piece of paper, or a keychain in them! You should also remove any jewelry or belts from the clothes.

8. Put the clothes in the washing machine one item at a time. Don't fill the machine; leave enough room for the clothes to move in soapy water.

9. Close the machine door and turn it on.

10. Once the cycle finishes, remove the clothes and put them in the dryer or hang them somewhere to dry.

11. Separate heavy fabrics from lightweights before you put them in the dryer.

12. When the clothes are dry, fold or hang them and put them in the closet.

Kitchen Skills

Who doesn't love to eat? Eating with your family is always fun. How about next time you surprise your parents by preparing dinner by yourself?

How about next time you surprise your parents by preparing dinner by yourself?
https://www.pexels.com/photo/women-holding-cooking-pan-7964684/

Simple Meal Preparation

Discover simple and delicious recipes to make for your family.

Lunch Box Pizza

Ingredients:

- 3/4 cup of shredded Monterey Jack cheese
- 10 pepperoni slices
- Italian seasoning
- ¼ cup of tomato sauce
- 10 refrigerated buttermilk biscuits

Instructions:

1. Get a big tray and put the biscuits on it.
2. Flatten each one into a circle shape, then press it into a greased muffin cup.
3. Put one teaspoon of Italian seasoning and tomato sauce in each cup, then add one tablespoon of cheese and a slice of pepperoni.
4. Put them in the oven at 425°F and let them bake for 10 to 15 minutes or until golden brown.
5. Take it out of the oven, and enjoy.

Chicken and Bacon Roll-Ups

Ingredients:

- 6 flour tortillas (room temperature)
- Fully-cooked crumbled bacon
- 1 cup of salsa
- 1 carton of spreadable vegetable cream cheese
- 1 can of chunk white chicken, drained

Instructions:

1. Mix ½ cup of salsa with bacon, cream cheese, and chicken, then spread over the tortillas.
2. Roll them up tightly, then put them in the fridge. Leave them for an hour.
3. Cut the tortilla into small pieces and serve with the remaining salsa.

Corn Dog Muffins

Ingredients:

- 2 tablespoons of pickled jalapeno, chopped, optional
- ½ cup of shredded cheddar cheese
- 5 sliced turkey hotdogs
- 1 lightly beaten large egg
- ⅔ cup of 2% milk
- 1 package of muffin/cornbread

Instructions:

1. Preheat the oven to 400°F and prepare nine muffin cups with foil liners.
2. Get a small bowl. Mix the egg, milk, and muffin/cornbread together, then add the jalapeno (if you want), cheese, and hotdogs.
3. Fill ¾ of the muffin cups with the ingredients and leave them to bake in the oven for 14 to 18 minutes.
4. After baking, let them cool down for five minutes. Remove from the pan and serve.

Brownie Batter Dip

Ingredients:

- Sliced apples or animal crackers
- M&Ms
- 1 teaspoon of vanilla extract
- 2 tablespoons of brown sugar
- ¼ cup of 2% milk
- ⅓ cup of baking soda
- 2 cups of sugar
- ¼ cup of softened butter
- 1 package of softened cream cheese

Instructions:

1. Beat the butter and cream cheese until smooth.
2. Add the vanilla, brown sugar, milk, cocoa, and sugar to the mix and beat until smooth.
3. Sprinkle the M&Ms and serve with the animal crackers or apple slices.

Yogurt and Honey

Ingredients:

- ¼ teaspoon of almond extract
- ½ teaspoon of grated orange zest
- 1 tablespoon of honey
- ¾ cup of vanilla or orange yogurt
- 4 ½ cups of your favorite fresh fruit like grapes, bananas, apples, and pears

Instructions:

1. Divide the fruit among six bowls.
2. Mix the almond extract with the orange zest, honey, and yogurt.
3. Spread the mix over the fruit and enjoy.

Frozen Banana Pops

Ingredients:

- 8 wooden pop sticks
- 4 peeled bananas cut in half
- 2 cups of any fruity cereal
- ¾ cup of strawberry yogurt

Instructions:

1. Put the cereal in one bowl and the yogurt in another.
2. Insert the pop sticks into the bananas, then dip them in the yogurt.
3. Roll the bananas in the cereal, then put them on a baking sheet.
4. Leave them in the freezer for one hour.

Setting the Table

1. Place a plate in front of each person on the dining table.
2. Put the cups on the top right of each plate.
3. Put clean napkins on each plate.
4. Place a spoon and knife on the right of each plate and a fork on the left.

Using Kitchen Appliances

Always be careful when using kitchen appliances.

- Ask your parents before using blenders, food processors, stoves, ovens, or knives.
- Always use oven mitts to hold baking trays or hot pans.
- Turn the pan and pot handles toward the back of the stove so you don't accidentally knock them over and hurt yourself.
- Don't use a gas stove by yourself. Ask your parents' assistance.
- Before using a microwave, ask your parents or Google if the cookware is microwave-safe. Don't use metal or tinfoil in the microwave.

Organizational Skills

No one likes a messy space. It can make you stressed and put you in a bad mood. Always keep your study area and personal space organized.

- Make your bed after you wake up.
- Take a look at your stuff and get rid of the things you don't use or have outgrown, like old toys or clothes that don't fit you anymore. You can even give them to charity.
- If you want to create more space, put your dresser in your closet.
- Clean up everything in your room and put it back in its place.
- Make it a habit to declutter your room occasionally and get rid of the things you don't need.
- Keep your desk tidy and remove anything that distracts you from studying. Only leave the things you'll need when doing your homework.

- Clean the garbage can in your room every day and remove the trash.

A clean room is an inviting room. When your room isn't cluttered or a mess, you will love spending time in it. You will also be able to focus while studying.

Time Management Tips

You may think you don't have time to do chores every day. You have school, studying, homework, practice, and a social life. Here is a secret – you always have time. The problem is you don't know how to manage it.

- Create a schedule and include everything you do throughout the day, like chores. You won't feel overwhelmed when you are organized and make time for all your tasks.
- If you have a few chores in one day, prioritize. Start with the most important first. So, if you feel tired or want to continue the rest tomorrow, you will be done with the most urgent ones.
- Set a timer for every chore so you can remain focused and finish them on time.
- Break down each chore into smaller ones so you don't get overwhelmed. For instance, if you are going to clean your room, focus on doing each part at a time.
- When you feel tired, take a break to relax.

Eco-Friendly Practices

Take care of your planet because you only have one.
https://unsplash.com/photos/green-plants-in-planter-on-wooden-surface-nCPpMv69m1s

If you take care of the environment, Mother Earth will take care of you. There are simple practices you can do every day to protect the planet.

- Turn off the lights whenever you leave a room
- Turn off the water when you are brushing your teeth

- After charging your cellphone, unplug the charger right away
- If you aren't using your laptop, turn it off or put it to sleep
- Don't use plastic or paper cups. Use reusable ones instead
- Rather than throwing your stuff away, swap them with your friends. Exchange items with each other
- Recycle items, like cans and plastic bottles, instead of throwing them in the trash. Tell your parents you want to recycle your stuff. Even if they aren't interested, tell them to just give them to you. You can put them in a recycling trash can and leave them on the curb, and an operative will take them. Recycling helps in reducing the amount of trash on the planet. Instead of throwing cans in the garbage, they can be turned into new ones.

Doing chores doesn't have to be boring or take much of your time. If you create and follow a schedule, you will finish your tasks quickly and can spend the rest of the day studying, relaxing, or doing whatever you want. You can always find ways to make them fun. You can listen to music while cleaning or compete with your siblings to see who will finish cleaning their room first.

Make household tasks enjoyable.

Section 10: More Useful Skills to Know

A few more skills would prove essential if you're looking to be self-sufficient and independent. The more you develop your skill set, the more self-aware you'll be. You'll make more sound and responsible decisions, become socially aware of your surroundings, and be able to manage any challenge thrown at you like a champ.

Staying Organized

Being organized limits the time you spend searching for things.
https://www.pexels.com/photo/sets-of-modern-stationery-on-table-5417630/

An easy way to stay organized is by utilizing technology, like setting up a calendar on your phone with reminders of important dates and tasks. You can catalog your photos, messages, and notes using separate apps and color-code them based on their priorities or urgency.

You can use Post-it notes (some call them "sticky notes") on a wall-mounted clipboard with to-do lists to help you keep track of what's important, what needs to be prioritized, and what can be pushed for later. There is nothing more satisfying than striking through a long list of chores.

Here's a simple rule: "A place for everything and everything in its place." Being organized limits the time you spend searching for things. Sectioning your belongings in different parts of the room and labeling them helps you remember where everything goes.

Try using physical organization tools, like closet and drawer organizers. These really come in handy if you want to section your makeup, accessories, or clothing items. They also make it less likely for you to throw the entire contents of your closet on your bed just to find one outfit.

Time Management

When you break down your day into specific timed tasks, you'll discover you can accomplish more in a shorter period. This essentially leads to you having much more free time to enjoy without any assignments hanging over your head.

As a result, you'll be more productive, and there will be a healthy balance between schoolwork and your personal life, allowing you to explore other interests.

Meeting deadlines is a skill you will need when you start working.

There are three steps to achieve time management:

- **Set Your Goal:** Figure out your endgame and break down the path to achieving it into bite-sized steps. The smaller the task, the easier it is to tackle it without procrastination(putting it off). Make sure that your goals are clear and attainable.

- **Prioritize Your Tasks:** Identify which tasks are urgent and which can wait. Which projects will take you a long time to finish, and which can be done quickly? Put your tasks in a list, starting with the highest priority to the least. This will help you focus your time and energy on one assignment at a time. Set aside an expected time to complete each task, and try your best to stick to it.

- **Stay Away from Distractions:** Turn your phone off or silence the notifications when you're working. Don't keep more tabs open on your computer than what's needed to complete your work. Find a quiet corner in the house away from any intrusions. If you start a task, stay with it until the end, and then take a short breather before starting the next one.

How to Read a Map and Use Public Transportation

Having the skill to navigate and read a map prevents you from feeling overwhelmed and lost in an unfamiliar area.

Make sure you know the four main directions, North, East, West and South. If possible, see if you can look up how to locate them using the sun and the stars. Pretend you're a pirate marooned on the sea, searching for your next treasure.

Familiarize yourself with the train and bus schedules in the area. Learn how to read the timetables for each of them.

Most importantly, test yourself. Pick a location you want to visit and check the maps and GPS for the best possible route. Consider speed, convenience, transportation, and toll prices when deciding the way you'll go.

How to Cope with Failure and Nurturing Resilience

Stress, strong emotions, and failure are all part of life. The key is not to let those feelings rule your existence. The more you experiment, the more you fail. And the more you fail, the more you learn and eventually succeed.

You must remember that you are only human, and humans are allowed and expected to make mistakes. Otherwise, you won't grow mentally or emotionally.

Do not put yourself down or allow others to do that. Examine the situation from all sides, see where it went wrong, and start working on improving it.

Focus on the positives of the outcome and what you've learned from it rather than dwelling on what should've or could've happened.

Listen closely to your self-talk and be gentle while speaking to yourself. Remember, if you wouldn't allow someone else to speak to you in a certain way, then don't do it to yourself.

Take a minute to collect yourself and breathe to avoid any rash decisions.

Before you react, first think about the expected consequences. Accept your anger and frustration. Don't try to push them aside or feel ashamed of them. It is perfectly normal to feel bad after a setback. Take some time to reset, do something you love to decompress, and talk to someone about how you feel, like a parent or a close friend.

Do a physical activity, like meditation or Yoga, to clear your mind. Ask for help if you're feeling overwhelmed, as a different perspective can help you see things in a new light.

Volunteering and Helping Others

There is no shortage of opportunities in society to help those in need.
https://unsplash.com/photos/people-picking-garbage-near-beach-PzQNdXw2a6g

Volunteering and helping others in your life aids your personal well-being and the community you live in.

When you give to others, you will feel a sense of pride and identity. It gives you a profound purpose.

There is no shortage of opportunities in society to help those in need. If you visit a local community center, church, school, or club, you will find places looking for volunteers to help.

Take a friend or a parent to keep you company at least the first few times. Having someone to share the experience with can deepen the bond between the 2 of you, not to mention all the new friends and connections you'll be making from the work itself.

Health Care and Basic First Aid

Prioritizing your health is a necessary habit you need to embrace. The more knowledgeable you are about treating yourself when faced with small medical challenges, the less likely you will feel sick for long.

- You need to know when to seek out a doctor, when an illness can be treated with over-the-counter medications, and when it's serious enough to require you to ask for help.
- Be aware of your environment, the weather, the seasons, whether it's that time of year when a lot of people catch colds or the flu.
- Ask your parents or a doctor about health insurance and vaccinations, how to get it, how to pay for it, and what it covers.
- Make sure you memorize the emergency number for medical support. Add a healthy diet to your daily routine. It's OK to treat yourself occasionally to sugary and fatty foods, as long as you don't overdo it and balance them out with healthy options. Exercise regularly to stay fit and lean.
- Familiarize yourself with the components of a first aid kit. Make sure that the one you have – wherever you find yourself (car, home, purse) is stocked with the required medications and bandages.
- Ask your parents to enroll you in a first aid class so you are prepared for any unexpected situations and to learn what to do in case of an emergency or injury. These lessons help you stay safe and potentially save others in need.
- Ensure your emergency contacts are updated with trustworthy individuals who will aid you when needed.
- Keep up with your routine health checks.

Using Basic Repair Tools and Crafting

Having an adult with you is preferred when learning about the different repair tools to avoid injury. It is helpful to know how to fix small malfunctions in your household and yield the required tools.

This habit comes in handy, especially with simple things such as tightening a screw or nailing a picture to the wall. Ask about the safest approach to handle each tool before using it. You'll also be less likely to stress out in the face of small challenges like cleaning a gutter, changing a lightbulb, resetting the circuit breaker, fixing a leaky faucet, or hanging shelves.

These small skills will make it much easier to manage your life when finally moving out of your parent's house.

Staying Safe and What to Do in an Emergency

Emergency drills are know-how practices you must memorize. Many natural disasters have occurred in recent years, including earthquakes, tsunamis, and hurricanes . . . are you ready for any of these?

In extreme situations, it is normal to feel stressed out. The key is to remain calm and maintain a clear mind.

- Start discussing the various dangerous possibilities with your parents or teachers. Make sure you have a "go bag" ready in case something happens.

- Go bags usually include protein snacks, flashlights, thermal blankets, extra cash, and other items necessary for surviving a challenging situation.

- Safety isn't only associated with disasters. Day-to-day challenges such as being on deserted roads alone, ending up on a highway, or being pursued by strangers need the same degree of level-headedness as dealing with a natural event.

- Have a close adult on speed dial – and make sure your phone is fully charged if you leave home. Don't be afraid to call out for help and make a loud noise if you feel threatened. Make sure that someone knows where you are at all times.

Goal Setting

The first step you take towards success is to have a goal set. The fun thing about goals is that they don't need to only include serious things, like studying and working. You can have extracurricular goals, personal relationships goals, physical health goals, and so much more.

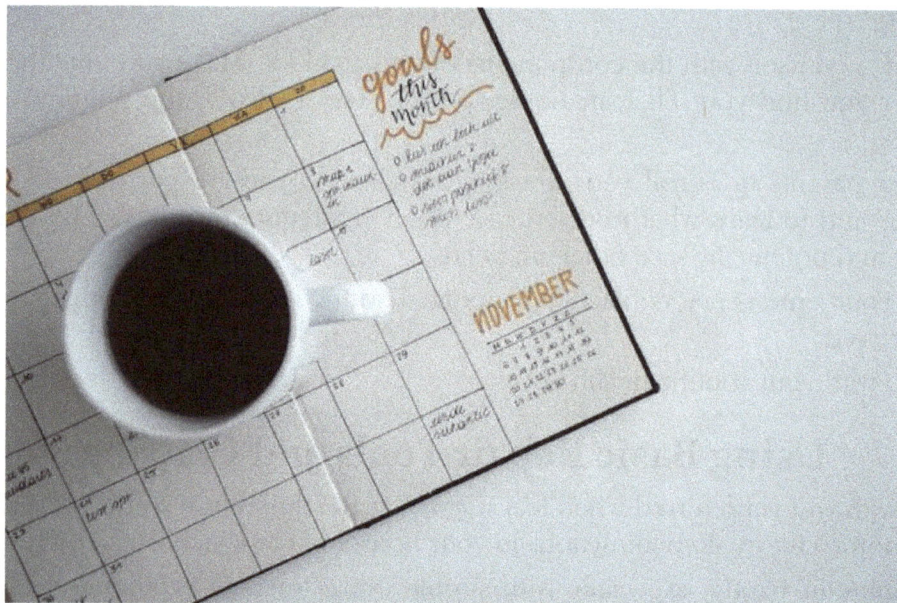

The first step you take towards success is to have a goal set.
https://unsplash.com/photos/white-ceramic-mug-with-coffee-on-top-of-a-planner-aQfhbxailCs

Ask yourself these questions:

- What is my goal?
- What skills do I have, and how can I use them to get where I want?
- Is there a course I can follow to achieve my end game?

As you figure out your goals, you'll get a general sense of direction on where you want to go next. If you focus on what you need and want, motivation will come easily. There are a few things to take into account when goal setting:

- **Make Sure You Have Specific, Measurable Goals**: Break down your goals into small milestones. You'll feel good about yourself as you reach each of those broken-down steps. Be sure to have a definitive way to measure your success and progress.
- **Make a Plan:** Start devising a plan of action with predetermined timelines so you stay focused on the target.
- **Be Accountable:** Take responsibility for setbacks. You should never berate yourself, especially if you stumble over things out of your hands. Just make sure you note when things get delayed or messed up and create a counter plan to avoid that happening again. Celebrating your successes by yourself and with family and friends is vital to keeping a motivated mindset. Having an accountability partner to keep you on your toes when you lose momentum is also a good idea.

Decision Making

As you grow up, you'll find that more and more, you're faced with tough decisions you have to make for yourself. Ask your parents to help you identify your values and ideals, the pillars on which you build most of your crucial decisions.

If you feel indecisive or pressured into a situation, list the pros and cons of the conclusion you're trying to reach. Find strong, positive role models and mirror their methods of handling hard decisions while maintaining your own moral compass.

- **Take into Account the Consequences:** Always look at the bigger picture. Don't focus on what's right in front of you but what could also potentially happen down the road!
- **Gather as Much Information as You Can:** Get your information from multiple sources. Don't rely on *one opinion.* Consult several trusted family members and friends.
- **Evaluate Your Options:** Once you have all the information, look at your alternatives. Weigh the pros and cons and see which decision is more likely to benefit you or, in some cases, cause the least possible harm. Take your time, and don't rush – rarely do impulsive decisions pay off.

Problem-Solving Skills and Critical Thinking

Seeking out help is great, but in some situations, you may need to stand on your own and do the math to get through it.

The best way to solve a problem is to work through it. Running away will do nothing for your confidence or your critical thinking abilities. Panic is a natural emotion, but you must master it with a solution-based mindset.

- **Listen Carefully:** Be an active listener. Understanding the problem and the root causes comes from examining the details you have at hand, and most of these details can be gathered from other people's perspectives. Not to mention, as you listen more, your communication becomes more efficient.

- **Break it Down:** Separate the problem into smaller parts. The smaller you go, the more manageable the issue. Take it one step at a time so you're not overwhelmed, and examine all the options carefully before jumping to conclusions.

- **Be Creative:** Ask around if someone else has faced a similar problem. Learning from other's mistakes helps you resolve your own issues. Think outside the box and brainstorm possible resolutions with people close to you. The more heads thinking together, the better the solution.

Employment Skills

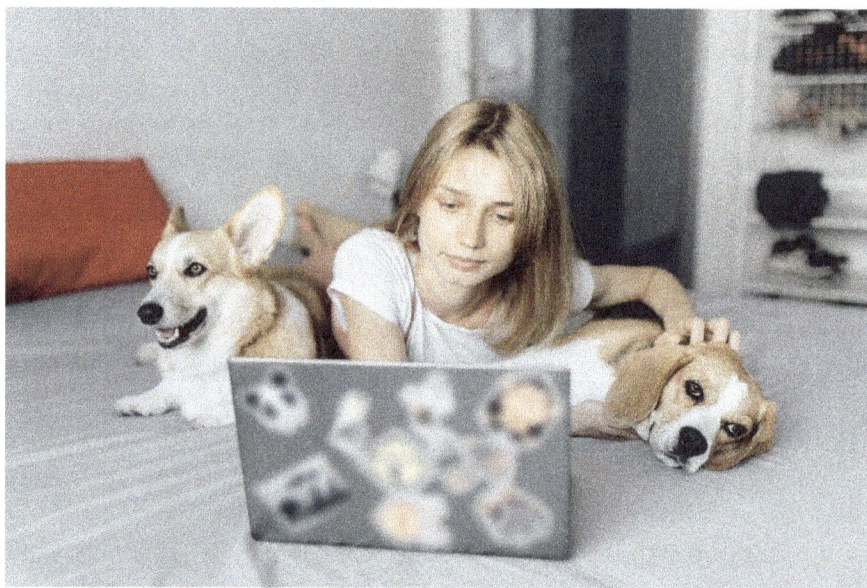

Start by making a resource.

https://www.pexels.com/photo/a-woman-petting-her-dogs-while-working-5122172/

Nothing prepares you for the outside world like looking for a job. As daunting as it may seem to find a job suitable for your age, it's not impossible. As you embark on this challenge, you'll find that your interpersonal relationships and self-management skills have improved.

Start by making a resume. Try not to overthink it, focus on your strengths, and don't compare yourself to others. Start practicing in the mirror for the interview. Ask your parents and peers who work what type of questions are usually asked, and put a creative twist on your answers.

Once hired, be punctual and follow the instructions carefully. Ask for consistent feedback to make sure you're not falling behind. And remember, at the end of the line, a payday is coming your way.

Basic Sewing Skills

Sewing is a practical skill most people don't pay much attention to. That's until you find a tear in your prom dress and have to be ready in 30 minutes! Do not lose your cool. Just because you've never sewn anything before does not mean it will be hard to start now.

Start with the simple approaches and work your way up:

Stitching Buttons

Begin with something uncomplicated – what to do if a button falls out. You'll need a needle, a thread, a button, and something to cut the thread with. If you're not home or happen to be on vacation, you can ask the hotel for an emergency sewing kit. Pick out the button that looks the most like the one you lost and a thread that matches the fabric's color.

How to Sew a Button

Pick out the button that looks the most like the one you lost and a thread that matches the color of the fabric.

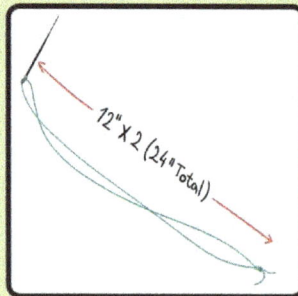

1. Prepare your needle with approximately 24 inches of thread. Pull it halfway through, ensuring equal lengths on both sides, and tie the loose ends together securely.

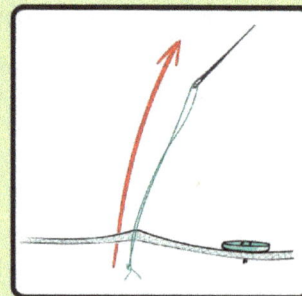

2. Begin on the back side of the fabric, threading the needle through and pulling the thread almost all the way.

3. Create a hash mark on the button side by returning the needle and thread through, forming an X. Repeat the process at a perpendicular angle for a secure hold.

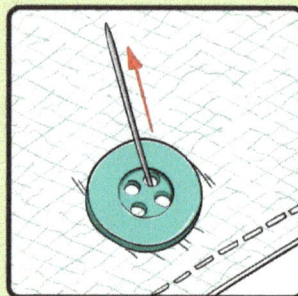

4. Position the button on the X mark. From the back side, pass the needle through one of the button holes.

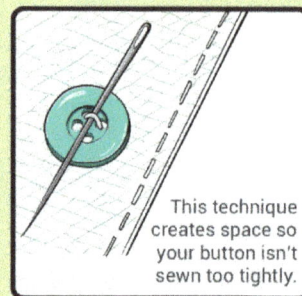

5. Use a spare needle or toothpick across the button to maintain space. Return the needle and thread through the opposite hole, pulling it taut.

This technique creates space so your button isn't sewn too tightly.

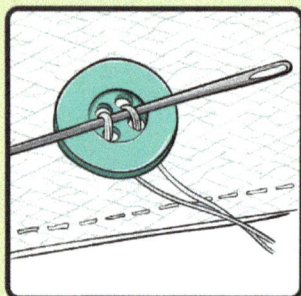

6. Continue sewing through the button holes, alternating between opposite holes. Always ensure the thread is pulled tight. Repeat this process for each set of holes three times.

7. Secure the button base by wrapping it tightly with a portion of the remaining thread. Aim for six tight loops around the base.

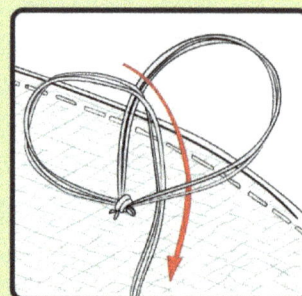

8. Pass the needle through to the back side of the fabric at the base of the button, pulling it taut. Tie it off with a simple overhand knot for a secure finish.

- Cut out a piece of thread, around 24 inches should do it.
- Thread the needle – pull the thread through the eye of the needle and double it over into two equal parts.
- Tie the ends of the thread together.
- Create an anchor point. Run the needle from the back end of the fabric into the front where the button will be, and then back and forth again. You want to create an X at the center where the button will be placed.
- Place the button on the anchor and start threading the needle starting from the back and through the 1st hole in the button.
- After pulling the thread through, push the needle back down through the opposite hole. You'll see that a single line is formed between the two opposing holes.
- Repeat the same process at least 6 times, leaving you with six passes, three for each set of holes in the button.
- On the sixth time, pull the thread through the front of the fabric but not the button. Pull the needle to the side and bring it around underneath the button. Create six loops around the threads at the bottom of your button. Pull tightly, then push the needle back from front to back and tie it up on the other end in a simple knot after cutting the thread.

Mending Small Tears

Mending tears depends on the type of tear and where it is. It can be a tear at the seam, an L-shaped tear, or a long rip, which is known as a clean rip, or a tear in a patterned fabric that can easily hide the fix you'll make.

Mending tears depends on the type of tear and where it is.

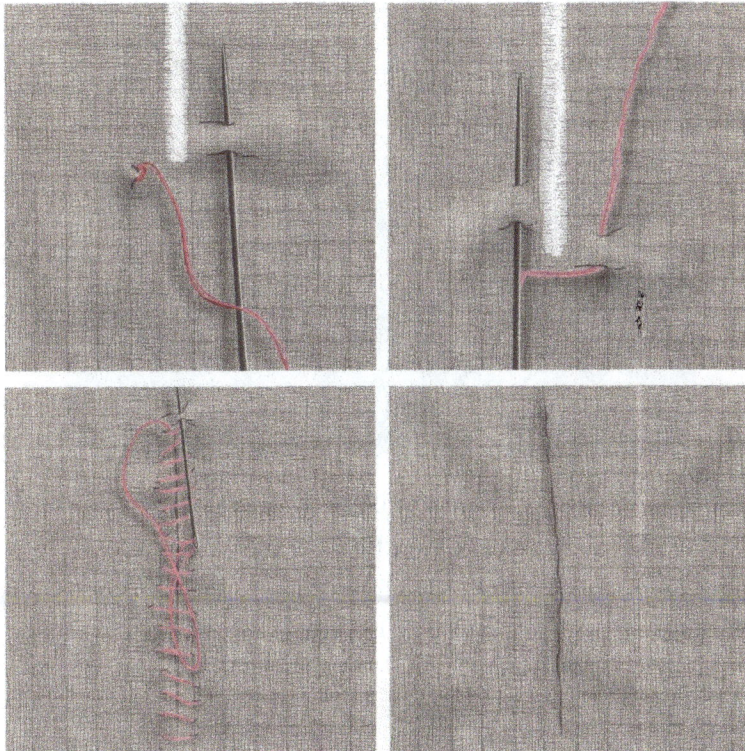

- Practice with the easiest one, the clean rip.
- Cut a thread of about 24 inches or longer if the rip is wider. Thread the needle as previously mentioned above.
- Make sure to iron the fabric and clean out any loose threads before you start. Be careful not to widen the hole while tidying the fabric.
- Insert the needle from the bottom of the fabric to the front. Make a small stitch to make sure the end is secured.
- Move the needle to the other side of the rip and make another small vertical stitch. Always try to make it as small as possible.
- Keep moving back and forth across the rip, making vertical stitches until you reach the top.
- Narrow the last stitches so they are pulled together.
- Very gently pull the thread. The rip will close, and the stitches will disappear.

Sewing on Patches

If the rip is too big or in the form of a hole, you'll need to patch it up.

- Start with tidying up the rip, as mentioned before.
- Select a patch, preferably from the same fabric and color. If you feel like experimenting, you can pick out a patterned patch. There is no rule that the whole garment should all look the same.
- Cut up the patch to the size of the rip and place it beneath the hole. Make sure that it's about 1 inch bigger than the hole from all sides.

- Pin it down. Secure it in place with pins or basting stitches.
- Start stitching around the torn area with a hand stitch.
- Tie up the ends of the thread and clean the reverse side by removing any excess fabric.

Self-Care

Learning basic skills of managing stressful situations or engaging in self-compassion and general healthy habits are key in facing the challenges thrown at you throughout your life.

- **Make Time for Yourself:** Carve out some alone time in your day to decompress. Do something you enjoy, like reading, walking, drawing, or even just taking a bath. The main thing is to relax and release any tension. Try as much as you can to make this a part of your routine.
- **Sleep:** Lack of sleep or messing with your natural schedule can throw your balance into a loop. If you don't sleep well or don't get enough sleep, you'll be groggy, tired, and unable to concentrate. Maintain a healthy sleep schedule to keep your internal clock regulated.
- **Stay Physical:** Do any physical activity within your weekly routine. Exercise releases Dopamine and Endorphins, the hormones that reduce stress and make you happy. Consider running, jumping around, swimming, or dancing – anything you enjoy doing. As long as you're moving, it doesn't matter what it is.

Standing Up for Yourself

There is a huge difference between being assertive and being rude and aggressive. Standing up for yourself isn't mean; it's being kind but firm at the same time. Set boundaries between yourself and others and ask them to respect them. Be clear on what you want and how you wish to be treated.

Practice with your friends how to be firm and look for kind, balanced ways to convey your message without falling into an aggressive mindset or a pushover one.

Having a Dress Sense and Clothes Skills

First impressions can last a while, but sometimes, it's hard to get past them. There is a term that says, "dress to impress," but the first person you need to impress is yourself. If you're comfortable with what you're wearing, it shows on your face, and everyone will see your confidence!

Pick out clothes that fit, not too loose, not too tight. If you're mixing colors in your clothing choices, try not to exceed three colors per outfit, and if there is a pattern, match the colors from it to the other articles of clothing.

Make sure your clothes are folded neatly in your closet so you don't end up with wrinkly fabrics when you need to wear them.

Ask other's opinions, but, in the end, remember that you have to approve, too. If everyone likes something you can't stand, follow your intuition and dispose of it.

Thank You Message

First, you need to give yourself a hefty pat on the back for your dedication and perseverance in completing this book. It takes a lot of effort to go through this amount of information (let alone learn it!), so you should be really proud of yourself.

You have learned the basics of some essential life skills that many adults struggle with. Not only that, but you've also taken your first steps towards independence and self-sustainability. Learning things, like managing your finances or acquiring a paying job, is how to lead a fulfilling life.

As you implement the techniques of self-care, critical thinking, and organizing your thoughts and space, you start to make the most of your time, making your existence more enjoyable and proficient.

Learning something like using transportation and reading maps won't just serve you in your hometown, but as you grow older and start traveling and exploring the world, this skill will help you ensure an enjoyable journey to see all the wonders on this Earth.

Growing your support system will provide companionship and enhance your communication skills.

Keep in mind your growth doesn't stop with these pages. People continue to learn as long as they are alive, and nothing can stop you from thriving once you put your mind to it. Once you've mastered these initial skills, start exploring others, like learning languages, leadership skills, and delving more into technology. You can find new ways to maintain your household or maybe learn how to plant a garden. You can expand on your self-care skills with more mindfulness techniques. Learn new recipes, find better study methods, and do your homework. Explore old-fashioned solutions like **snail mail** or learn the responsibilities of keeping a pet.

The sky's the limit. The only thing that can stop you from learning is your own mind and imagination. So, keep your mind as open as can be, and remember you're not competing with anyone but yourself.

Check out another book in the series

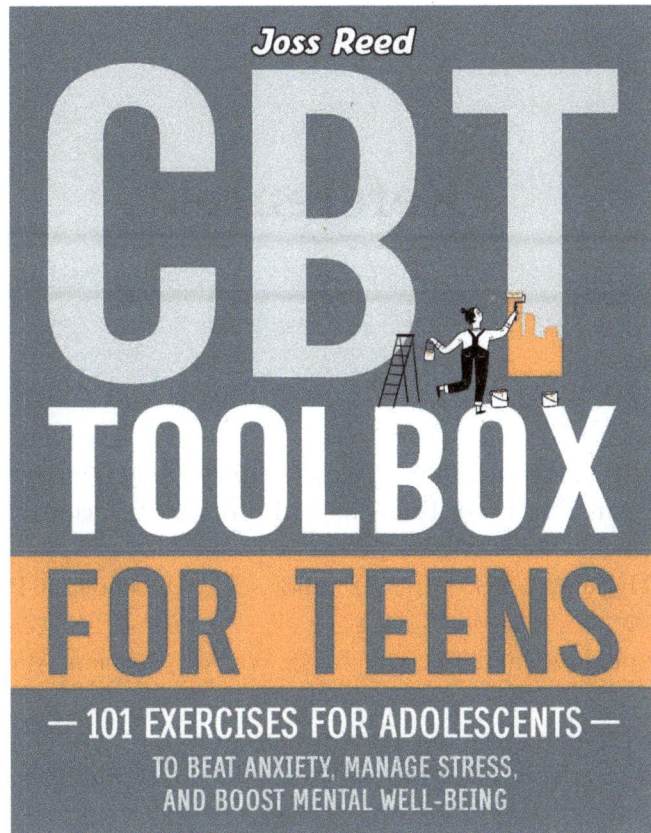

References

(N.d.-a). Child-encyclopedia.com. https://www.child-encyclopedia.com/sites/default/files/emotions-info.pdf

(N.d.-b). Cfctherapy.com. https://cfctherapy.com/5-calming-techniques-to-help-children-regulate-their-emotions/?cn-reloaded=1

(N.d.). Gohenry.com. https://www.gohenry.com/us/blog/financial-education/teaching-teens-about-money-management

(N.d.). Masterclass.com. https://www.masterclass.com/articles/value-of-friendship#4eZSD1Dg30Zq4V83IndD4e

10 Essential Life Skills for Teens That Every Teen Should Learn. (2022, October 24). HIGH5 Strengths Test; HIGH5 TEST. https://high5test.com/life-skills-for-teens/

10 Ways to Teach Preteen Hygiene. (2019, April 10). Scholastic.com; Scholastic Parents. https://www.scholastic.com/parents/family-life/kids-health/10-ways-to-teach-preteen-hygiene.html

24 Life Skills Every Teen Should Learn. (2023, March 14). We Are Teachers; WeAreTeachers. https://www.weareteachers.com/life-skills-for-teens/

25 Affirmations for Resilience. (2017, April 24). Thefocusonyou.com.

4 Reasons Why You Should Mop Your Floor Regularly. (n.d.). Leifheit (Singapore). https://leifheit.sg/blogs/leifheit-cleaning-blog/4-reasons-why-should-mop-your-floor-regularly

5 Reasons Why Recognising Your Emotions Is Important. (2019, September 30). BBC. https://www.bbc.co.uk/teach/five-reasons-why-recognising-emotions/z7gxjhv#:~:text=Recognising%20your%20emotions%20and%20learning,manage%20difficulties%20and%20set%20backs.

8 fun and easy ways to teach kids about friendship. (2023, May 22). Begin Learning. https://www.beginlearning.com/parent-resources/friendship-kids/

9 essential life skills for teens. (2023, June 12). Global Citizen Year. https://www.globalcitizenyear.org/content/life-skills-for-teens/

A guide to time management for kids. (n.d.). Orchids. https://www.orchidsinternationalschool.com/blog/social-skills/tricks-to-teach-time-management

Aba, H. T. (2017, August 29). 4 ways to teach initiating conversation. How to ABA. https://howtoaba.com/teach-kids-initiating-conversation/

Ackerman, C. E., MA. (2023). What Is Self-Confidence? (+ 9 Proven Ways to Increase It). PositivePsychology.com. https://positivepsychology.com/self-confidence/

Adele, T. (2023, July 31). 4 expert-backed breathing exercises for anxiety. Forbes. https://www.forbes.com/health/mind/breathing-exercises-anxiety/

Aguirre, S. (2006, December 14). How to sweep a floor. The Spruce. https://www.thespruce.com/how-to-sweep-a-floor-1901115

Ajani, L. (2012, January 4). How to take good care of your body (for tween girls). WikiHow. https://www.wikihow.com/Take-Good-Care-of-Your-Body-(for-Tween-Girls)

Amy Morin, L. (2012, August 5). The importance of chores for kids. Verywell Family. https://www.verywellfamily.com/the-importance-of-chores-for-kids-1095018

Antonio. (2019, June 10). How to sew on a button. The Art of Manliness; Art of Manliness. https://www.artofmanliness.com/skills/how-to/sewing-on-a-button/

Arlin Cuncic, M. (2022) 7 active listening techniques to practice in your daily conversations, Verywell Mind. Available at: https://www.verywellmind.com/what-is-active-listening-3024343 (Accessed: 05 October 2023).

Baker, K. (2023, September 6). 30 Positive Affirmations for Confidence - UWS London. UWS London. https://www.uwslondon.ac.uk/mental-health/positive-affirmations-for-confidence/

Barnard, D. (2022) Examples of positive and negative body language, VirtualSpeech. Available at: https://virtualspeech.com/blog/examples-positive-and-negative-body-language (Accessed: 05 October 2023).

Be a green kid. (n.d.). Kidshealth.org. https://kidshealth.org/en/kids/go-green.html

Being safe in the kitchen. (n.d.). Kidshealth.org. https://kidshealth.org/en/kids/safe-in-kitchen.html

British Heart Foundation (2023) 10 tips for active listening, BHF. Available at: https://www.bhf.org.uk/informationsupport/heart-matters-magazine/wellbeing/how-to-talk-about-health-problems/active-listening (Accessed: 05 October 2023).

Broom Guru. (n.d.). 9 important benefits of sweeping the floor. Broom Guru.

Brownie batter dip. (n.d.). Taste of Home. https://www.tasteofhome.com/recipes/brownie-batter-dip/

Bryant, C. D. (n.d.). What is empathy? Talking with Trees Books. https://talkingtreebooks.com/teaching-resources-catalog/definitions/what-is-empathy.html

Cheddar corn dog muffins. (n.d.). Taste of Home. https://www.tasteofhome.com/recipes/cheddar-corn-dog-muffins/

Chicken & bacon roll-ups. (n.d.). Taste of Home. https://www.tasteofhome.com/recipes/chicken-bacon-roll-ups/

Chrissy. (2022, September 20). 50 affirmations for self-compassion to change your life. Fun Loving Families.

Common Sense Media. (2020, June 2). What is communication? Common Sense Media. https://www.commonsensemedia.org/articles/what-is-communication

Confidence (for Teens) - Nemours KidsHealth. (n.d.). https://kidshealth.org/en/teens/confidence.html

Conway, S. (2021, January 17). Name it to tame it: How labelling emotions helps kids manage them. Mindful Little Minds Psychology. https://www.mindfullittleminds.com/name-it-to-tame-it/

Cooks-Campbell, A. (n.d.-a). Breathwork: The secret to emotional regulation. Betterup.com. https://www.betterup.com/blog/breathwork

Cooks-Campbell, A. (n.d.-b). Triggers: Learn to recognize and deal with them. Betterup.com. https://www.betterup.com/blog/triggers

Dellner, A. (2017, June 30). How to vacuum like a pro in five easy steps. PureWow. https://www.purewow.com/home/how-to-vacuum

Demme Learning. (2022, December 6). 6 essential life skills for teens to learn before leaving the nest. Demme Learning. https://demmelearning.com/blog/life-skills-teens/

Deshpande, S. (2018, January 25). 10 Reasons Why Household Chores Are Important. 1SpecialPlace. https://1specialplace.com/2018/01/25/importance-household-chores/

Elizabeth Scott, P. (2023a) 5 simple steps to assertive communication, Verywell Mind. Available at: https://www.verywellmind.com/learn-assertive-communication-in-five-simple-steps-3144969#toc-how-to-develop-an-assertive-communication-style (Accessed: 05 October 2023).

Elizabeth Scott, P. (2023b) 5 simple steps to assertive communication, Verywell Mind. Available at: https://www.verywellmind.com/learn-assertive-communication-in-five-simple-steps-3144969#toc-how-to-develop-an-assertive-communication-style (Accessed: 05 October 2023).

Empowering children with positive beliefs. (2018, July 1). Parenta.com. https://www.parenta.com/2018/07/01/empowering-children-with-positive-beliefs/

Engler, B. (2023) Teaching your child to deal with conflict – Connections Academy®, – Connections Academy®. Available at: https://www.connectionsacademy.com/support/resources/article/building-conflict-resolution-skills-in-children/ (Accessed: 05 October 2023).

Erin Johnston, L. (2022) How using 'I feel' statements can help you communicate, Verywell Mind. Available at: https://www.verywellmind.com/what-are-feeling-statements-425163#toc-examples-of-i-feel-statements (Accessed: 05 October 2023).

Essential life skills for 16-year-Olds. (2019, September 17). Summerlin Hospital. https://www.summerlinhospital.com/about/resources/caring-for-kids-and-teens-online-fall-2019-september/essential-life-skills-16-year-olds

Feldman-Barrett, L. (n.d.). We don't understand how emotions work. A neuroscientist explains why we often get it wrong. Sciencefocus.com. https://www.sciencefocus.com/the-human-body/what-are-emotions

Friends lyrics by I'll Be There for You by the Rembrandts from Television/TV Theme Lyrics - 80's, 90's soundtrack. (n.d.). Stlyrics.com. https://www.stlyrics.com/lyrics/televisiontvthemelyrics-80s90s/friends.htm

Friendships: Enrich your life and improve your health. (2022, January 12). Mayo Clinic. https://www.mayoclinic.org/healthy-lifestyle/adult-health/in-depth//art-20044860

Frozen banana cereal pops. (n.d.). Taste of Home. https://www.tasteofhome.com/recipes/frozen-banana-cereal-pops/

Gongala, S. (2014, July 25). 21 essential life skills for teens to learn. MomJunction. https://www.momjunction.com/articles/everyday-life-skills-your-teen-should-learn_0081859/

Guest Blogger. (2014, November 5). Teach kids to set the table in 5 simple steps. Education Possible. https://educationpossible.com/teach-kids-to-set-the-table-5-simple-steps/

Habits, B. M. (2023, September 19). The 5 most important financial lessons for teens. Better Money Habits; Bank of America. https://bettermoneyhabits.bankofamerica.com/en/personal-banking/money-management-for-teens

Hansen, E. (2022, October 11). 6 tips for raising resilient and confident girls during adolescence. Local Anchor. https://localanchor.com/tips-for-raising-resilient-and-confident-girls

Hartney, E., & MSc, M. A. (2009, August 29). What is peer pressure? Verywell Mind. https://www.verywellmind.com/what-is-peer-pressure-22246

Healthdirect Australia. (2022). Personal hygiene for children. https://www.healthdirect.gov.au/personal-hygiene-for-children

Helping your children find their passion. (n.d.). Kudoswall.com. https://kudoswall.com/index.php/easyblog/entry/5-ways-of-helping-your-child-find-their-passion

Household chores for children and teenagers. (2023, April 5). Raising Children Network. https://raisingchildren.net.au/preschoolers/family-life/routines-rituals-rules/chores-for-children

How to read body language and gain deeper emotional awareness (no date) BetterUp. Available at: https://www.betterup.com/blog/how-to-read-body-language (Accessed: 05 October 2023).

How to teach growth mindset to children (the 4-week guide). (n.d.). Big Life Journal. https://biglifejournal.com/blogs/blog/teach-growth-mindset-kids-activities

How to Teach Your Child Body Positivity. (n.d.). Mental Health America. https://www.mhanational.org/blog/how-teach-your-child-body-positivity

How your child's beliefs about themselves shape their future success. (n.d.). The New Age Parents. https://thenewageparents.com/child-beliefs-shape-future-success/

Huang, E., CFA, CFP®, & CPA. (n.d.). 10 money management tips for teens. Echo Wealth Management. https://www.echowealthmanagement.com/blog/10-money-management-tips-teens

Hunter, J. (n.d.). Encouraging a growth mindset. The GiST. https://www.thegist.edu.au/families/getting-them-interested-in-stem/encouraging-a-growth-mindset/

Hygiene: pre-teens and teenagers. (2021, April 23). Raising Children Network. https://raisingchildren.net.au/pre-teens/healthy-lifestyle/hygiene-dental-care/hygiene-pre-teens-teens

Iannelli, V. (2007, August 9). How kids make and keep friends. Verywell Family. https://www.verywellfamily.com/making-and-keeping-friends-2633627

Indeed, Editorial Team. (2022, June 25). Top 15 Traits of Successful People. Indeed.com. https://www.indeed.com/career-advice/career-development/trait-of-successful-people

Jannes, M. (2011, May 26). How to be a hygienic teenage girl. WikiHow. https://www.wikihow.com/Be-a-Hygienic-Teenage-Girl

Jones, H. (no date) What are social cues?, Verywell Health. Available at: https://www.verywellhealth.com/social-cues-5204407#toc-what-are-social-cues (Accessed: 05 October 2023).

Jordan, T. (2014, January 5). Feeling machines: Healthy ways for girls to express their emotions. Pittsburgh Parent. https://www.pittsburghparent.com/feeling-machines-healthy-ways-for-girls-to-express-their-emotions/

Juni Learning. (2022, August 10). 25 important life skills for teens to learn - Juni learning. Junilearning.com. https://junilearning.com/blog/guide/important-life-skills-for-teens/

Kerr, J. (2023, June 23). How to mop floors, including tile, hardwood, laminate, and more. Better Homes & Gardens. https://www.bhg.com/how-to-mop-7511534

Key strategies to teach children empathy (sorted by age). (n.d.). Big Life Journal. https://biglifejournal.com/blogs/blog/key-strategies-teach-children-empathy

Kojic, M. (n.d.). How to set SMART goals (+ examples and templates). Clockify Blog. https://clockify.me/blog/productivity/smart-goals/

Kristen. (2020, February 16). Girls hygiene helpers. Busy Kids Happy Mom. https://www.busykidshappymom.org/tween-girl-hygiene-helpers/

Kristenson, S. (2023, March 15). 11 SMART goals examples for time management & productivity. Develop Good Habits; S.J. Scott. https://www.developgoodhabits.com/smart-goals-time-management/

Kruse, K. (2020, October 19). How to raise girls with A grit and growth mindset. Forbes. https://www.forbes.com/sites/kevinkruse/2020/10/19/how-to-raise-girls-with-a-grit-and-growth-mindset/

Langston, G. (2023, February 11). Strengths and weaknesses - Help your teen discover theirs. College Flight Plan. https://collegeflightplan.com/strengths-and-weaknesses-help-your-teen-discover-theirs/

Leverette, M. M. (2015, July 9). How to do laundry in 10 easy steps. The Spruce. https://www.thespruce.com/how-to-do-laundry-2146149

Lorioswald. (2022). Learning to Positively Respond to Constructive Criticism from Professors. Post University. https://post.edu/blog/how-to-take-constructive-criticism/

Lunch box pizzas. (n.d.). Taste of Home. https://www.tasteofhome.com/recipes/lunch-box-pizzas/

Making friends. (n.d.). LeapFrog. https://www.leapfrog.com/en-us/learning-path/activities/making-friends-with-sash-role-play

Mendler, A. (2013, November 5). Teaching your students how to have a conversation. Edutopia; George Lucas Educational Foundation. https://www.edutopia.org/blog/teaching-your-students-conversation-allen-mendler

Mikhail, A. (2022, October 6). Self-affirmations can improve your confidence. Here's how to start. Fortune Well. https://fortune.com/well/2022/10/06/self-affirmations-can-improve-your-confidence-heres-how-to-start/

Miller, M. (2019, February 18). 9 ways to teach A growth mindset to kids. Six Seconds. https://www.6seconds.org/2019/02/18/9-ways-to-teach-a-growth-mindset-to-kids/

Money management for teenagers. (2023, March 16). Raising Children Network. https://raisingchildren.net.au/pre-teens/family-life/pocket-money/money-management-for-teens

Morin, A. (2019, August 5). Conversation tips for kids who struggle with social skills. Understood. https://www.understood.org/en/articles/conversation-tips-kids-social-skills

Natalie Watkins, M. S., Morin, D. A., & Viktor Sander B. Sc., B. A. (2022, September 13). I-statements: How & when to use them (with examples). SocialSelf. https://socialself.com/blog/i-statements/

Neff, D. (2022). Tips for Kids on How To Nail Presentations in the Classroom. Duarte. https://www.duarte.com/tips-for-kids-to-nail-presentations/

No title. (n.d.). Com.Eg. https://www.twinkl.com.eg/teaching-wiki/emotion

No title. (n.d.). Homemadesimple.com. https://www.homemadesimple.com/in-the-home/learn-how-to-mop-in-just-five-steps/

O'Donnell, J. (2009, February 13). Teaching kids hygiene habits to last a lifetime. Verywell Family. https://www.verywellfamily.com/kids-hygiene-and-your-tween-3288310

PHC. (2021, September 24). Health benefits of vacuuming. PHC Service. https://www.phcvacuumservice.co.uk/health-benefits-of-vacuuming/

Philippines, E. (2022, December 1). How to use vacuum cleaner: 7 easy steps. Electrolux Philippines. https://www.electrolux.com.ph/blog/how-to-use-vacuum-cleaner/

Reid, S. (n.d.). Empathy: How to feel and respond to the emotions of others - Helpguide.org. https://www.helpguide.org/articles/relationships-communication/empathy.htm

Riserbato, R. (2021, March 2). 4-step skincare routine 11 year Olds. Kidskin. https://kidskin.com/blogs/news/four-step-skincare-routine-for-11-year-olds

Sara Bean, M. E. (2011, July 18). Behavioral triggers: How to find the ones that set your kid off. Empowering Parents. https://www.empoweringparents.com/article/how-to-find-the-behavioral-triggers-that-set-your-kid-off/

Sinha, R. (2021, August 5). 27 irreplaceable and important qualities of A good friend. MomJunction. https://www.momjunction.com/articles/qualities-of-a-good-friend_00761023/

Smith, R., Alkozei, A., & Killgore, W. D. S. (2017). How do emotions work? Frontiers for Young Minds, 5. https://doi.org/10.3389/frym.2017.00069

Stevens, T. (2019, April 3). Dusting 101: How to dust properly and why it's so important. Sparkle and Shine. https://www.sparkleandshine.today/blog/dusting-101-how-to-dust-properly-and-why-its-important/

Stressed out? be assertive (2022) Mayo Clinic. Available at: https://www.mayoclinic.org/healthy-lifestyle/stress-management/in-depth/assertive/art-20044644 (Accessed: 05 October 2023).

Teaching children empathy. (n.d.). TheSchoolRun. https://www.theschoolrun.com/teaching-children-empathy

Tefl, M. G. M. M. A. (n.d.). Helping girls to embrace a growth mindset. Girlsschools.org. https://www.girlsschools.org/wp-content/uploads/2018/07/Breakout-Session-F_Helping-Girls-to-Embrace-at-Growth-Mindset.pdf

The Counseling Teacher. (2019, July 31). 8 healthy friendship qualities to teach students. Confident Counselors. https://confidentcounselors.com/2019/07/31/healthy-friendship-qualities/

The difference between coherence and cohesion in writing. (2022, February 15).

The Empeople Daily. (2019, June 6). 6 real money lessons every parent should teach their teenager. Empeople. https://empeople.com/learn/empeople-insights/6-real-money-lessons-for-teens

The key to independence: 8 life skills for teens. (n.d.). Positiveaction.net. https://www.positiveaction.net/blog/life-skills-for-teens

The value of friendships. (n.d.). Com.au. https://www.zurich.com.au/latest-news/magazine/my-wellbeing-hub/the-value-of-friendships.html

Treasurie. (2023, June 5). How to sew a rip - best way to sew a tear or holes. Treasurie. https://blog.treasurie.com/how-to-sew-a-rip/

Understanding your emotions. (n.d.). Kidshealth.org. https://kidshealth.org/en/teens/understand-emotions.html

Valamis (2023) 4 types of communication: Verbal, non-verbal, written, visual, Valamis. Available at: https://www.valamis.com/hub/types-of-communication (Accessed: 05 October 2023).

Washing clothes and bedding. (n.d.). Housing for Health - the Guide. https://www.housingforhealth.com/the-guide/health-housing/washing-clothes-and-bedding/

Williamson, N. (2021, May 20). How to explain and teach empathy to a child. As They Grow. https://www.as-they-grow.com/how-to-explain-and-teach-empathy-to-a-child

Wong, D. (2023, April 14). 15 essential life skills for teens (does your teen have them?). Daniel Wong. https://www.daniel-wong.com/2023/04/14/life-skills-for-teens/

Yogurt & honey fruit cups. (n.d.). Taste of Home. https://www.tasteofhome.com/recipes/yogurt-honey-fruit-cups

www.ingramcontent.com/pod-product-compliance
Lightning Source LLC
Chambersburg PA
CBHW081419090426
42738CB00017B/3417